Trust and you will See
Believe and you will Know
have Faith, all is Well
Follow your Heart
and Spirit will Lead you

~ Dawna Campbell

Also by Dawna Campbell

Financially Fit

*Living the Secrets to an Abundant
and Prosperous Life*

**The Art of Connection, Volume 4,
with Robert Jones**

*365 Days of Gratitude for Business Owners,
Entrepreneurs, and Influencers*

Courses:

**The Financially Fit Transformation
The Infinite Prosperity System
Create it Now**

THE ABUNDANT SOUL

*Creating Inner Wisdom
or Financial Success*

Dawna Campbell

@copyright 2024 Dawna Campbell

Published and distributed in Gifts Of Legacy LLC: Scottsdale, Arizona.

All rights reserved. No part of this publication may be reproduced, distributed, or transmitted in any form or by any electronic or mechanical means, including information storage and retrieval systems, without written permission from the publisher or author, except in the case of a reviewer who made quote brief passages embodied in critical articles or in a review.

Although the author and publisher have made every effort to ensure that the information in this book is correct at press time, the author and publisher do not assume and, with this, disclaim any liability to any party for any loss, damage, or disruption caused by errors or omissions, whether such errors or admissions result from negligence, accident, or any other cause.

KDP Ebook - ASIN : B0CSQQ3JFV

KDP Print - ISBN: 979-8-9898500-4-4

KDP HardBack - ISBN: 979-8-9898500-5-1

IngramSpark Print - ISBN: 979-8-9898500-6-8

IngramSpark Ebook - ISBN: 979-8-9898500-7-5

Library of Congress:

@2024 Dawna Campbell - All rights reserved

GIFTS OF
Legacy

This book has been written with the assistance of a sophisticated literary AI prompt developed by Ernesto Verdugo. If you are interested in utilizing a prompt like this to aid in writing your book, please feel free to contact Ernesto Verdugo at ernesto@ernestoverdugo.com

DEDICATION

For 'The Medicine Woman'
who always
loved a good heart felt laugh in
the comedy we call life.

ACKNOWLEDGMENTS

As I reflect upon the incredible journey of creating "The Abundant Soul," I find it difficult to express the depth of my gratitude for the multitude of people who have played a significant role in bringing this book to life. While it's impossible to name everyone, I want to acknowledge some extraordinary individuals who have been instrumental on this path of abundance.

Jana Short, your unwavering belief in me and your encouragement to write "The Abundant Soul" has been an invaluable gift. Your profound guidance, wisdom, expertise, and unwavering faith in my vision have fueled my determination.

Moe Rock, I want to express my deepest gratitude for the countless conversations and unwavering support you've provided throughout this project, helping to manifest my vision. Your contributions have far exceeded any words I could use to convey my appreciation.

Ernesto Verdugo, I extend my heartfelt gratitude for your integral role with the creation of "The Abundant Soul." Your presence, training, and dedication to this process have been instrumental; bridging together the missing links.

Misty Kerrigan, you have been a true inspiration, and your support has touched every aspect of this project. You are the best manager, coach, mentor, accountability strategist, encourager, publicist, sounding board, believer, and friend that a person could ever dream of.

My heartfelt thanks extend to my dedicated and incredibly patient team members, Natalie McQueen, Buddy Thornton, Eric Yaillen, and Aaftab Sheikh, who have been indispensable in bringing "The Abundant Soul" to fruition. Your contributions are deeply appreciated.

Sherry Gideons, your assistance and connections have been an integral part, and I'm grateful for your generous support.

Bob Doyle, your thoughtful foreword and words about "The Abundant Soul" have added depth and meaning to this book. Your contribution is genuinely cherished and I thank you for sharing your thoughtful words.

To my close friends and family members, you have been a constant source of love. Your presence in my life is a blessing beyond words, and I'm grateful for each of you.

Last but certainly not least, I'd like to remember Oberon with fondness. His memory remains a cherished part of this journey. Until we meet again my friend.

To all those whose names I couldn't include here, please know that your contributions and support have not gone unnoticed. Your presence in my life has been a tremendous source of inspiration.

TABLE OF CONTENTS

Foreword by Bob Doyle, Featured Teacher in The Secret xii

Author's Note xvii

Chapter 1: Shattered Reality 1

Chapter 2: Return to Reality 15

Chapter 3: Shadows of the Corporate Ladder 29

Chapter 4: A Cup of Friendship 39

Chapter 5: Crossroads of Reflection 53

Chapter 6: A Leap of Faith 61

Chapter 7: Balancing Act 71

Chapter 8: The Coin of Emotions 83

Chapter 9: A Swanky Evening 99

Chapter 10: The Power of Duality 109

Chapter 11: In Search of Answers 123

Chapter 12: Synchronistic Opportunity 135

Chapter 13: Countdown to Transformation 147

Chapter 14: Exploring the Mind-Body Connection 157

Chapter 15: Confronting the Shadow Within 173

Chapter 16: The Money Dance of Emotions 189

Chapter 17: The Subconscious Shift 199

Chapter 18: Endings and New Beginnings 211

Chapter 19: The Fourth Side 223

Chapter 20: Buddha of Inner Abundance 237

Meet the Author. 247

Foreword by Bob Doyle, Featured Teacher in The Secret

As someone who has studied the remarkable capacities of the human mind for over 20 years, it was a joy to dive into the pages of The Abundant Soul. This insightful book chronicles the journey of protagonist Kristol as she awakens to the power of her emotions and cultivates inner abundance.

I recognize many familiar concepts from my own teachings on manifestation and utilizing the principles of The Secret. However, Dawna Campbell brings a refreshing, soul-centered perspective to conscious creation with this narrative. Through Kristol's eyes, we are reminded that external wealth originates from nurturing our inner riches like self-love, joy, and intrinsic self-worth.

The Abundant Soul provides an accessible, step-by-step framework for learning emotional awareness and attracting prosperity. A powerful section details Kristol's time at a transformative retreat led by the skilled teacher Stuart. The immersive exercises at the retreat mirror tangible techniques I share with my own students.

For instance, participants engage in journaling to excavate their fears and limiting beliefs around money. This reflective process allows them to extract and examine self-sabotaging patterns. They then practice elevating their energetic vibration from lower states like anxiety to higher frequencies such as inner abundance. This emotional transmutation shifts their energetic output to attract prosperity rather than push it away.

What I find compelling about The Abundant Soul is how the conceptual teachings are woven into the narrative itself. When Kristol collaborates with her mentor Citta, she taps into higher wisdom through meditation and inner reflection. Her consistent journaling helps integrate lessons and represents her changing relationship with finances. Even her purchase of a symbolic Buddha statue sparks valuable self-examination.

While the mind-body mechanics of vibration and the subconscious fascinated me, this story succeeds by rooting principles in emotional transformation. As someone versed in the teachings of the heart, I believe we are guided from this realm of pure feeling. Kristol's journey bears testament to how profoundly our emotions shape our lives.

It has been an honor to walk with Kristol as she embraces the infinite well of potential within herself. Any reader will feel moved by her courage to inhabit the deeper layers of self. She illuminates how our outer world blossoms when we nurture the garden of our inner landscape.

I am thrilled to recommend this book to anyone seeking to welcome more abundance by attuning to their highest vibrational state. The Abundant Soul reminds us that wealth lies quietly within all of us, ready to unfold at the right moment. Dawna Campbell has gifted us all by sharing this uplifting tale of emotional healing and financial freedom.

Bob Doyle
Featured Expert in "The Secret"

AUTHOR'S NOTE

It fills my heart with immense joy to have the opportunity to share the wisdom that has been derived from my role as a financial advisor and my tenure as a managing principal in the world of investments, but also from the transformational experiences that have shaped me into a catalyst for personal transformation and healing.

"The Abundant Soul" is a self-help novel that builds upon and applies the principles introduced in my first book, "Financially Fit: Living the Secrets to an Abundant and Prosperous Life." Within these pages, you will discover a deeper exploration of those teachings, aimed at helping you unlock your true potential and achieve financial abundance.

It's important to note that everything shared in this book is not limited to its pages. I am dedicated to sharing these lessons through courses, transformative retreats, and exclusive private sessions. The wisdom within "The Abundant Soul" is a living, breathing philosophy that extends beyond the confines of this novel.

My greatest hope is that you not only enjoy the teachings presented in these pages but also find the inner wisdom to guide you on your path to financial success. I encourage you to savor the knowledge within this powerful book and, if you find value in it, to share it with your cherished family and friends. Together, we can empower others towards a life of infinite abundance.

With Happiness, Prosperity, and Love,

Dawna Campbell

Chapter One

SHATTERED REALITY

The harsh combination of car horns and the relentless crawl of rush hour traffic created a suffocating atmosphere as Kristol inched her way home in her sedan. Each honk vibrated through her, a constant reminder of the impatience that permeated the city's veins. Her heart raced like a wild horse, skipping beats with each passing second.

With each inch forward, the tension in her body mounted, and her grip on the steering wheel tightened. The sun dipped below the horizon, casting long shadows over the maze of cars. Her weary eyes, heavy from a grueling day at the office, blinked slowly, trying to stay focused on the brake lights ahead. Little did she know, this routine evening commute was about to transform her life.

Suddenly, as if summoned by fate, the world around her exploded. A deafening screech of tires pierced the air. In an instant, a blinding flash of headlights illuminated the enclosed space of her car, washing everything in a stark, ghostly white.

Time seemed to be standing still, frozen in eternity. The forceful impact sent shockwaves of pain and fear coursing through her body.

Metal scraping against metal, the sound of glass shattering, Kristol's world circled into chaos. Her sedan spun uncontrollably. Gravity abandoned Kristol, with a sensation of weightlessness overwhelming her senses. The world outside her windshield was a blur of twisted metal and a kaleidoscope of colors, bringing confusion and disorientation.

The blaring sirens of emergency responders in the distance penetrated through the turmoil. Kristol's senses struggled to make sense of the calamity unfolding. Her world fell into an eerie silence. This heart-stopping moment would forever alter the course of Kristol's life. In those fleeting moments, her life flashed before her eyes.

Kristol, a single woman in her early 40s, had always been a dedicated soul. Her career as a corporate trainer demanded her unwavering commitment, and she had given it willingly. She was an overachiever, pouring her talents and abilities into her work, hoping that her loyalty would lead to the recognition and financial abundance she craved.

The corporate world had proven to be a challenging landscape. Despite her best efforts, her talents remained unnoticed, undervalued, and unappreciated by those on the executive team. The frustration of giving it her all without acknowledgment had worn her down, leaving her exhausted and overworked.

As Kristol lay in the wreckage, drifting into unconsciousness, she couldn't help but feel the weight of her unmet aspirations. Her dreams of financial success, once so vivid, seemed to be slipping through her fingers. A growing sense of scarcity and lack replaced the childlike wonder and awe she once possessed. The pursuit of success, the relentless climb up the corporate ladder, and the unfulfilled dreams haunted her.

Fully unconscious, Kristol found herself suspended in a realm beyond the familiar boundaries of her existence that defied the ordinary laws of reality. Colors became alive with an intensity she had never imagined, each hue more vibrant and surreal, as if painted by the hand of an otherworldly artist.

Emotions became living, breathing, tangible energies. It was as though she had stepped into a place where thoughts and feelings took material shape, where the very essence of her being manifested into life. Thoughts, fueled by emotions and feelings, held the power to create the world around her. Her inner world blended with the external, intricately woven together. Her consciousness was alive, and the external world responded in this suspended state.

Kristol found herself surrounded by endless flowers casting a radiant glow that illuminated her with an ethereal light. She was floating effortlessly among these blossoms, their fragrances intoxicating. The air was filled with the gentle whispers of the petals, their secrets and wisdom flowing through her senses.

Kristol's thoughts and feelings were intimately interconnected with the flowers that surrounded her. Her inner world had found a mirror, where every emotion, every sentiment, and every fleeting thought manifested itself through the flower petals. When her heart filled with joy and gratitude, the petals of the flowers responded in kind, radiating vivid colors and a luminous glow, dancing to the vibrations of the harmony of her emotions.

Conversely, when moments of doubt and uncertainty passed through Kristol's mind, the flowers mirrored her turmoil. Their petals would quiver, their colors dimmed and reflected the shadows that momentarily clouded her thoughts. When fear arose within Kristol, the flowers wilted, turning black and shriveling up.

As abruptly as it had begun, the dreamlike interlude ended. Kristol's eyelids fluttered open, and her surroundings shifted to the stark reality of a hospital room. The sterile white walls and the rhythmic beeping of machines greeted her, a sharp distinction from the dream world she had just experienced.

As her groggy consciousness awakened, Kristol was struggling to make sense of her reality. She could hear the doctors and nurses in the background, her body aching and her head throbbing with pain. Slowly, her bleary eyes focused on two familiar figures by her side. The first was her mother, Evelyn, who possessed a firm and unwavering demeanor.

Evelyn had always been resolute in her principles, instilling a sense of discipline and responsibility in her children. Her expectations were clear, and she held them to high standards. Beneath that stern exterior, there were moments of deep love and affection. Evelyn's love for her children sometimes was over-expressed by worry and protection. In moments of vulnerability, her children could catch glimpses of the tender-hearted mother who would embrace them warmly and offer words of encouragement.

Beside Evelyn stood her older sister, Emily, who exuded an air of confidence and ambition. Emily's presence was a sharp distinction to Kristol's. She glanced at Kristol with a mix of concern and determination, her competitive nature ever-present even in this challenging moment.

Kristol's heart swelled with surprise, and apprehension washed over her. Evelyn's presence offered comfort and reassurance, while Emily brought a sense of sibling rivalry that had been a part of their relationship for as long as she could remember.

Evelyn spoke first, her voice filled with a blend of relief and worry. "Kristol, you gave us quite a scare. How are you feeling?"

Kristol's throat felt dry, and her words came out in a raspy whisper. "I...I'm not sure, Mom. What happened?"

Emily chimed in, her concern evident in her words. "Don't worry, Kristol. You're going to be okay. The doctors said it was a miracle you survived that crash."

Evelyn, her voice filled with relief, "Oh, sweetheart, you were in a car accident. But you're going to be okay. The doctors said you need some rest."

Kristol nodded weakly, her mind still grappling with the surreal transition from the dreamlike realm to the reality of the hospital room. "I don't even know what happened. It was like...like a dream."

Evelyn reached out and gently stroked Kristol's forehead. "You don't have to worry about that now, dear. The important thing is that you're here with us, safe and sound."

"Mom, Emily," Kristol began, her voice shaky in disbelief, "I was in a car accident?"

Her mother, her eyes brimming with tears, nodded gently. "Yes, sweetheart, you were. But you're here now, and you're going to be all right."

Kristol's brow furrowed as she tried to piece together the fragments of her recollections. "I remember the crash, the impact... but then, there was something else. It was like... like I was in a different place, surrounded by flowers and colors I've never seen before."

Kristol's mother, gently placing a hand on her daughter's, reassured her once again, "Kristol, darling, don't worry about that now. We'll figure out the details of what happened later. Right now, we're just grateful that you're okay."

Emily, with a hint of superiority in her tone, chimed in, "But we should definitely talk about what's next. Your job, the car, all those details... Don't worry, I've got this. We'll work through it together."

Emotions spiraled in Kristol's head. The accident had brought her face-to-face with her family, and it was clear that their dynamics hadn't changed much. Her mother's well-intentioned love and concern, seemingly oblivious to Emily's realistic approach and competitive nature, only added to the underlying tension that remained unchanged between them all.

"Honey," Evelyn spoke gently, "let me go get the doctor and tell him that you're awake." Kristol lay in her bed, feeling vulnerable and disoriented, with Emily by her side. She took slow, shallow breaths, still attempting to make sense of the situation.

Turning her attention to her older sister, her voice still scratchy, "Em, I appreciate your help, but what do you mean about 'what's next?'"

Emily regarded her sister thoughtfully, though a hint of a smirk played at the corner of her lips. Her initial concern for Kristol's well-being now mingled with a sense of empathy and understanding. She leaned closer to Kristol, her tone seemingly sincere, but there was a subtle dig in her words. "Kristol, I get it. We all have unique paths in life, and sometimes, we need to reassess where we're heading."

Kristol couldn't help but wonder if Emily's concern was genuine or if there was more to her sister's motivations than met the eye. Her accident had exposed the complexities of their relationships, leaving Kristol to navigate. Kristol considered how to express herself when the door swung open; Evelyn walked in, followed by a tall doctor wearing glasses and a nurse carrying a clipboard.

"Kristol, this is Dr. Patel," her mother explained, "he is a neuroscientist." He approached Kristol's bedside with authority, his warm smile attempting to put her at ease.

"Good evening, Kristol," Dr. Patel began in a soothing tone. "I'm Dr. Patel, and this is Nurse Patricia Becker. We're here to take care of you and make sure you're on the road to recovery."

Nurse Becker efficiently began to check Kristol's vitals, attaching monitors and asking routine questions about her medical history. Kristol complied, feeling a sense of relief.

Dr. Patel turned his attention to Kristol with his gentle eyes, "Now, Kristol, I understand this must be quite overwhelming for you. Can you tell me what you remember about the accident?"

Kristol's brows furrowed as she tried to recall the last moments before losing consciousness. "It all happened so fast," she began, her voice trembling slightly. "I remember the screeching tires, blinding headlights, and then...everything went dark."

Dr. Patel nodded sympathetically. "That's understandable, Kristol. What you experienced was a traumatic event, and it's not uncommon for your memory to be a bit fuzzy. We'll piece together the details over time."

While Nurse Becker continued her work, Dr. Patel proceeded to ask Kristol a series of questions about her physical state. He inquired about her level of pain, any loss of consciousness, or memory lapses. Kristol answered as best she could, though her recollection was hazy.

"I remember," Kristol started, "there were all these flowers around, vibrant and alive. But when I opened my eyes, I was in this room."

Dr. Patel, however, remained focused on his medical chart, barely glancing in Kristol's direction. "That's interesting, Kristol," he replied in a detached tone, "you may be experiencing hallucinations brought on by the trauma of the accident. We will get you some medication for that. But right now, our focus should be on your recovery and ensuring your well-being."

He spent the next several minutes examining Kristol's reflexes, checking her eyes and nervous system responses with meticulous precision. Kristol followed his instructions, her anxiety slowly giving way to trust in his expertise. Each test felt like a small victory as he confirmed that her neurological functions appeared normal. After a thorough examination, Dr. Patel consulted with Nurse Becker, reviewing Kristol's vitals and test results. He then turned back to Kristol, his expression compassionate.

"Kristol," he began gently, "I want to be upfront with you. You've sustained a concussion with some brain swelling and bruising. Additionally, you have a broken leg. I must say, given the severity of the accident, you are incredibly fortunate to be alive. The probabilities, based on the pictures of the crash, don't fully account for your survival."

Kristol's eyes widened as the news of her situation sank in. She had always considered herself lucky, but this was beyond anything she could have imagined.

Dr. Patel continued, "We'll be monitoring your condition closely. You'll need rest and time to heal. Nurse Becker here will ensure you're comfortable and receive the necessary care." The nurse nodded; her demeanor was professional yet gentle.

Dr. Patel continued, his tone softening. "Kristol, you have a long road ahead of you, but I have every confidence that you will recover. You've already defied the odds." With a reassuring smile, "You've been making remarkable progress, and your vitals look excellent. However, to be on the safe side, we'd like to keep you for a few more days of observation. If everything continues to check out and your condition stays stabilized, you should be able to be discharged soon. We want to monitor her closely and make sure there are no complications." Dr. Patel's words were delivered with a mix of professional expertise and genuine concern for Kristol's well-being, looking at her mother.

Evelyn nodded, her expression projecting a mix of relief and concern. "Of course, Doctor. We want what's best for Kristol."

Emily interjected, "What about after she's discharged? What's the plan for her recovery?"

Dr. Patel turned his attention to Emily, appreciating her forward-thinking approach. "That's an excellent question, Emily. Once Kristol leaves the hospital, she will need ongoing rehabilitation for her broken leg. This will likely involve physical therapy and exercises to regain strength and mobility."

Kristol's heart sank at the thought of a prolonged recovery process, but she knew it was a necessary step toward returning to a sense of normalcy.

Dr. Patel continued, "Rehabilitation will be a gradual process, and it may take several months for Kristol to fully regain her strength and mobility. There were several breaks. It's essential that she follows a structured plan to ensure the best possible outcome."

Evelyn placed a reassuring hand on Kristol's shoulder, her motherly concern evident. "We'll be there every step of the way, won't we, Kristol?"

Kristol managed a weak smile, grateful for her family's unwavering support. "Yes, Mom, Emily, I appreciate you both being here for me."

Dr. Patel concluded the discussion with a note of encouragement. "Kristol, you've already shown incredible resilience. I do not doubt that you'll make a strong recovery. It won't be easy, but remember, every small step forward is a victory."

Kristol nodded, her gratitude making it difficult to find words. "Thank you, Dr. Patel."

The doctor's eyes twinkled with a hint of thoughtfulness, "I want to stress the importance of taking your recovery seriously. The brain is a remarkable organ, but it needs time to heal. And your leg, too, will require patience and dedication during rehabilitation."

Evelyn and Emily exchanged a silent glance, silently acknowledging the challenges that lay ahead. They were prepared to support Kristol, ensuring that her journey toward recovery was as smooth as possible.

He proceeded to outline the next steps. As Dr. Patel spoke, the nurse continued monitoring Kristol's vitals. The steady beeping of the machines provided a comforting backdrop to their conversation.

"I understand," Kristol replied, determination in her eyes.

Over the next few days, Kristol found herself feeling more alert, her strength returning. Dr. Patel returned with a smile, pleased with her progress. "Kristol, I'm happy to inform you that everything is looking great. Your vitals are stable, and the tests show no concerning signs. It's time for you to head home."

Dr. Patel offered some final words of advice. "Remember, Kristol, your body has been through a lot. Be patient with yourself during your recovery. If you experience any unusual symptoms or have concerns, don't hesitate to reach out to us or your primary care physician."

Kristol nodded, grateful for the news. The nurse arrived shortly afterward, prepared with the discharge paperwork and a bag of necessary medications. She carefully explained each prescription, outlining the dosages and any potential side effects. Kristol listened attentively, determined to follow the medical instructions to the letter.

As Kristol sat in the hospital room, waiting for the discharge paperwork to be processed, she couldn't help but reflect on the experience she had gone through. The accident had been a wake-up call, a reminder of how fragile life could be.

Her mind wandered back to the moments after the crash, the world of flowers transforming into something beyond her comprehension. The boundaries of existence seemed to blur and bend, and she found herself in a place where the ordinary rules of reality no longer applied.

Kristol experienced a sense of interconnectedness, a oneness with the universe that transcended the limitations of her everyday life. It was a place where her deepest fears and desires had manifested before her, forcing her to confront the truths that had been buried within her subconscious.

As she waited to leave the hospital, waiting for her mom to arrive, Kristol couldn't help but wonder about the significance of that other world. What had it meant? What had it revealed about her innermost thoughts and beliefs? And most importantly, how would it impact her life moving forward?

As the nurse returned with the completed discharge paperwork, Kristol knew that she carried with her a new sense of purpose and a determination to explore the depths of her consciousness. The accident had been a catalyst for change, a gateway to a world of possibilities she had never imagined. --And she was ready to embrace the journey ahead with an open heart and a curious mind.

Chapter Two

RETURN TO REALITY

After leaving the hospital, Kristol and her mother, Evelyn, headed back to Kristol's cozy condo. The ride home was filled with relief and uncertainty. Kristol couldn't help but think about the accident and the strange dreamscape she experienced while unconscious.

Once they arrived, Evelyn helped Kristol settle in. The condo was filled with warm, earthy tones and an abundance of natural light. It had always been a place of comfort for Kristol, but now it felt even more like a sanctuary.

With crutches in hand, Kristol carefully made her way to her favorite spot near the large window overlooking the city. She had a few days off before her expected return to work, and there were some paperwork matters to attend to.

Sitting in her plush armchair, Kristol turned her attention to the stack of papers on the coffee table. They were a mix of medical forms, insurance documents, and accident reports. Going through them felt like wading through a sea of bureaucracy.

As she reviewed the paperwork, Kristol couldn't help but think about how life could change in an instant. She had always been someone who thrived on structure and planning, but this unexpected turn of events had shaken her sense of control.

Evelyn brought over cups of coffee and sat down next to Kristol. "You know, Kristol, accidents happen, and we can't always predict or prevent them."

Kristol sighed, her gaze fixed on the documents in front of her. "I know, Mom, but it's just... everything happened so quickly. I still can't believe it."

Evelyn reached out, "It's natural to feel overwhelmed, especially after what you've been through. But you're a strong and resilient woman. You've overcome challenges before, and you'll do it again."

Kristol managed a small smile, appreciating her mother's unwavering support. "Thanks, Mom. I guess I just need some time to process all of this."

Evelyn took a deep breath and fixed her gaze firmly on Kristol. "You know, dear, from the moment you were born, I've always seen something special in you. You have a fire within you, a drive to achieve and strive for the top. I've always believed in your potential, and I still do. This accident, as challenging as it is, shouldn't deter you from your path."

Kristol was moved by her mother's words, her eyes welling up with tears. "Mom, I appreciate your faith in me. But right now,

I'm not sure. It's like I've been given a wake-up call, and I'm not entirely sure what it's trying to tell me."

Evelyn maintained her stern expression. "Kristol, let me be clear. I expect you to rise above this setback, just as you've risen above every obstacle in the past. You have a bright future ahead of you, and I won't accept anything less than your best effort to achieve it."

Kristol decided to ignore her mother's comments and shifted the conversation away from her expectations, focusing on practical matters. She knew she had a doctor's appointment coming up to monitor her healing leg, and there were also arrangements to be made regarding the rental car through her insurance company.

"Speaking of getting back on my feet, Mom, I have my doctor's appointment tomorrow; he wants to make sure my leg is healing well," Kristol mentioned, trying to sound cheerful despite the circumstances.

Kristol continued, "And I need to get in touch with the insurance company about the rental car. It'll be a relief to have some mobility again."

Kristol picked up the phone and dialed the number provided by the insurance agent to obtain a rental car. While she navigated the automated menu and waited on hold, the door to her condo opened, and her sister Emily walked in with her two dogs, Max and Bella. The dogs immediately ran into the living room, their tails wagging furiously in excitement.

"Kristol!" Emily exclaimed, rushing over to give her sister a warm hug. "I'm so glad to see you're back home. How are you feeling?" Kristol returned her sister's hug with a smile. "I'm hanging in there, Em. It's good to be back, though."

Emily took a step back and looked at Kristol with concern, her demeanor different than the few days before at the hospital. "I can't believe you had to go through all of this. It must have been terrifying."

"It was," Kristol admitted, her voice tinged with emotion. "But I'm trying to focus on healing and moving forward."

Emily nodded in understanding and glanced at the crutches leaning against the wall. "You've got some company to keep you entertained now." She gestured to Max and Bella, Kristol's two dogs, who were now playfully wrestling on the carpet.

As they caught up, Kristol's call to the insurance company finally connected.

"Hello, this is Kristol Davis," she said as she greeted the agent on the line. "I'm calling about the rental car arrangement for my accident claim."

The agent confirmed her details and informed her that the rental car had been reserved and would be available for pick-up the following day. Kristol thanked the agent and hung up, feeling relieved that she would soon have a way to get around independently.

"It looks like I'll have a rental car by tomorrow," Kristol shared with Emily. "That should make things a bit easier."

Evelyn's eyes sparkled with excitement as she said, "That's wonderful news about the rental car, Kristol! I can take you to pick it up and accompany you to your doctor's appointment."

Her mother's offer genuinely touched Kristol. "Mom, that would be a huge help."

Evelyn waved off her daughter's gratitude. "Of course, dear. Family takes care of each other. Besides, it'll be good for us to spend some time together. We can make a day of it."

Kristol smiled warmly at her mother's enthusiasm. "That sounds like a plan, Mom. And maybe afterward, we can grab lunch or something."

Evelyn nodded in agreement. "Absolutely. We'll turn it into a little mother-daughter outing."

Emily's gaze fixed on Kristol with a determined intensity. "So, Kristol, what's your plan for going back to work? What's next on your list of achievements?"

Kristol's brow slightly furrowed as she met her sister's probing eyes. She had expected Emily's curiosity and knew that her sister had always been driven and goal-oriented. However, the question made her head spin. The accident had shifted her perspective, and she was still trying to find her footing in this new phase of her life.

"Well," Kristol began cautiously, "I'm still healing, Em. My focus right now is on regaining my strength and mobility. Going back to work is on the horizon, but I need to take it one step at a time."

Emily's impatience was noticeable as she leaned back in her chair. "Kristol, you've always been ambitious, always striving for the top. You can't let this setback hold you back. You should be setting new goals, reaching for new heights."

Kristol sighed, her gaze drifting to the window as she contemplated her sister's words. Emily was right; she had always been a high achiever, someone who set lofty goals and worked tirelessly to reach them. But after her accident and the experiences she had in that otherworldly realm, her priorities had shifted.

"I know, Em," Kristol replied softly. "But I need some time to figure things out."

As the day continued, Evelyn and Emily prepared to leave, and Kristol exchanged warm goodbyes with her mother and sister.

Just as they were stepping out the door, Kristol's phone rang. She checked the caller ID and smiled as she answered, "Hey, Sarah!"

Sarah's cheerful voice came through the phone. "Hey, Kristol! How are you feeling?"

Kristol settled back into her chair, crutches by her side. "Getting better every day."

"That's great to hear," Sarah replied. "I've been thinking about you a lot. I was wondering if you're up for some company."

Kristol's eyes brightened. She had missed her best friend's company during her hospital stay. "Of course, Sarah! I'd love to see you. Are you free to come over?"

"Absolutely," Sarah replied. "I can be there in about 30 minutes. I'll bring some Chinese food, and we can catch up."

Kristol's heart warmed at the thought of spending time with Sarah. "That sounds wonderful. See you in a bit!"

Sarah, Kristol's best friend, had met years ago while working at the corporation. Their friendship had flourished into a deep and lasting connection. Sarah was known for her boundless enthusiasm and bubbly personality, traits that seemed to provide a never-ending source of energy. She had a contagious zest for life that could be both exhilarating and, at times, exhausting.

With her chestnut brown hair always perfectly styled, Sarah exuded confidence and charm. She had a knack for fashion and knew how to dress appropriately for any occasion. Whether it was a corporate meeting or a casual get-together, Sarah always seemed to have the perfect outfit.

Despite her external appearance of having it all together, Sarah had her quirks. She was a little on the plump side, but her athleticism and energetic nature made it easy for her to maintain a healthy lifestyle. Sarah was the type to offer advice and wisdom to her friends, often giving valuable insights into various aspects of life. However, she had a tendency not to follow her own advice, a trait that amused Kristol and was the source of many inside jokes between them.

Kristol cherished her friendship with Sarah. They balanced each other out in many ways, with Kristol's calm and thoughtful nature providing a grounding influence on Sarah's exuberance. Together, they made a dynamic duo, supporting each other through the ups and downs of life.

As the doorbell rang, Kristol knew it could only be one person – her best friend, Sarah. With a warm smile, she hobbled over to answer the door, using her crutches for support. Max and Bella sensed Sarah's arrival and were dancing around in excitement.

"Hey there, Kristol!" Sarah greeted her with her trademark enthusiasm as she entered the condo, carrying a bag of Chinese takeout.

"Sarah, you have no idea how much I've been craving Chinese food!" Kristol said, her eyes lighting up as she smelled the delicious aroma wafting from the bag.

"Thought you might be, so I brought your favorite," Sarah replied with a grin, placing the food on the dining table. Max and Bella circled around her, tails furiously wagging as if they knew she always brought treats for them.

Kristol chuckled as she watched her dogs' antics. "You two are such attention hounds when Sarah's around."

Sarah knelt to give Max and Bella some well-deserved pets. "Can't resist these cuties, can I?"

With the dogs now momentarily appeased, Kristol and Sarah settled at the dining table, ready to enjoy their meal. They chatted about work, upcoming events, and the latest happenings in their lives. Sarah had a talent for turning even boring topics into lively conversations, and Kristol couldn't help but be swept up in her friend's contagious energy.

"So, Kristol," Sarah began between bites of fried rice, "how are you feeling? Any updates on your recovery?"

Kristol took a moment to sip her coffee before responding. "Well, I've got an appointment with my doctor tomorrow to check on my leg. And I've been dealing with the insurance company to get a rental car while they figure out the adjustments on mine for a new car.

Sarah nodded in understanding. "It's good that you're taking care of all that stuff. You've got to make sure you're back on your feet soon."

Kristol hesitated for a moment before deciding to share something with her friend. "You know, Sarah, while I was in the hospital, I had this strange experience. It was like I was in a different world, surrounded by flowers. Everything felt so vivid and intense. And then, I woke up in the hospital room."

Sarah raised an eyebrow, her curiosity piqued. "That does sound strange. Like a dream or something?"

Kristol nodded. "Yeah, except it felt more real than a dream. It's hard to explain, but it was almost like... another reality."

Sarah gave her friend an encouraging smile. "Well, Kristol, you've always had a vivid imagination. Maybe it was just your brain playing tricks on you while you were unconscious."

Kristol wasn't entirely convinced, but she decided to let it go for now. "Maybe you're right. Anyway, it's good to have you here, Sarah. Your energy always brightens my day."

As Kristol and Sarah finished their Chinese food, they eagerly reached for the fortune cookies that had come with their order. Sarah cracked hers open first and giggled at the message inside.

"Mine says, 'Adventure is just outside your window.' How fitting!" Sarah exclaimed, her eyes sparkling with excitement.

Kristol smiled at her friend's enthusiasm but couldn't help feeling a sense of anticipation as she held the fortune cookie in her hand. She broke it open and carefully extracted the slip of paper, her heart racing slightly.

She unfolded the small piece of paper and read the message silently to herself first, then out loud. It simply said, "Embrace happiness, for your feelings shape the world you see."

Sarah raised an eyebrow, intrigued by the significance Kristol attached to the message. "That's interesting. What do you think it means?"

Kristol stared at the fortune cookie message for a moment, her mind filled with uncertainty. She then looked at Sarah with a thoughtful expression and admitted, "You know, Sarah, I don't know."

After their dinner, Sarah bid Kristol goodbye. She hugged her best friend tightly and promised to check in on her soon. As

Sarah left, Kristol felt a sense of warmth and gratitude for having such a supportive friend in her life.

The next morning began with Evelyn's early arrival. She was eager to assist Kristol with her appointments and errands. They had a busy day ahead, including a visit to the doctor's office and picking up the rental car.

Kristol and Evelyn arrived at HealthCare Link, her general practitioner's office, where she was scheduled to see Dr. Baker. The waiting room was quiet, with a few other patients sitting in chairs, scrolling through their phones. Kristol feeling a combination of anxiety and relief, anticipating her check-up.

When Kristol's turn came, Dr. Baker greeted them warmly and began to examine her leg. After carefully inspecting the healing process and reviewing her X-rays, he smiled and delivered some positive news.

"Well, Kristol," Dr. Baker said with a kind smile, "I'm pleased to report that your leg is healing remarkably well. It looks like you've been taking good care of yourself."

Kristol couldn't help but breathe a sigh of relief. She had worried about potential complications or setbacks in her recovery, but it seemed that her dedication to following the doctor's orders had paid off.

Dr. Baker nodded. "You can start putting more weight on your leg now, but take it slow and don't push yourself too hard."

Evelyn beamed with pride at her daughter's progress. "That's wonderful news."

"Kristol, you've made excellent progress," Dr. Baker continued, "and I believe you'll be ready to go back to work next Monday. Of course, continue to use the crutches as needed, and if you experience any discomfort, don't hesitate to contact me."

Kristol was pleasantly surprised by the news. She had been eager to get back to her job, and this development was a step in the right direction. "That's fantastic, Dr. Baker! Thank you so much."

After leaving the doctor's office, Kristol and Evelyn decided to grab a quick bite to eat at a local taco joint. They both had an appetite and thought some tasty tacos would hit the spot.

As they walked into the cozy restaurant, the enticing aroma of grilled meat and spices enveloped them. The place was bustling with activity as people chatted and enjoyed their meals. Kristol and Evelyn found an empty booth and settled in.

Kristol ordered her favorite chicken tacos, while Evelyn chose the beef. Sharing some lively conversation over delicious meals, they discussed family matters, upcoming summer plans, and Kristol's progress in her recovery. It felt good to spend time together, savoring the simple joys of life.

Once they had satisfied their appetites, it was time to tackle the next item on their agenda—picking up the rental car. They left the restaurant and headed to the rental car agency, where they were greeted by a friendly attendant who quickly processed the paperwork. Soon, Kristol was behind the wheel of a comfortable rental car.

After a busy day, Kristol returned home, exhausted. She carefully parked the rental car and made her way inside, leaning on her crutches for support. The day's activities had taken a toll on her healing leg, and she was looking forward to some much-needed rest. Her condo, with its familiar and comforting surroundings, welcomed her back.

Kristol eased herself onto the couch, propping her leg up on a soft cushion. She closed her eyes for a moment, taking a deep breath and savoring the quiet solitude of her home. It felt good to be back in her own space, where she could relax and recharge. With her leg comfortably elevated and her dogs by her side, Kristol closed her eyes once more, ready to drift into a well-deserved rest.

Chapter Three

SHADOWS OF THE CORPORATE LADDER

Monday morning arrived, and Kristol was back in the heart of the towering skyscrapers of the financial district. The city's ceaseless bustle surrounded her, the car horns and the rush of people on their way to work serving as a constant reminder of the life that she had returned to.

As the familiar surroundings of the office building came into view, its cold, imposing exterior gave Kristol chills. A sinking feeling settled in the pit of her stomach. The corporate world, with its unending demands, loomed over her like a shadow.

Kristol had dedicated herself to her career as a corporate trainer, pouring her heart and soul into her work, hoping that her efforts would finally lead to the recognition and financial success she craved.

As she entered the office building, the sterile, fluorescent-lit hallways seemed to reflect the coldness of her current reality.

The faces of her colleagues, lost in their own worlds, barely acknowledged her presence. It was a clear indication that in the corporate world, everyone was too consumed by personal ambitions to foster genuine connections.

As she settled into her desk, surrounded by the hum of ringing phones and the click of keyboards, Kristol couldn't shake the feeling that something profound had shifted within her. The accident was a wake-up call, a reminder that life is too precious to be spent in pursuit of empty success and recognition.

As she stared at the computer screen before her, Kristol couldn't help but wonder if it was time to chart a new course, explore the depths of her own mind, and seek a different kind of abundance. She couldn't shake the feeling that there was something meaningful about the car accident, something that called out to her amidst the monotony of her daily routine.

Her thoughts turned to her best friend, Sarah, who had been a constant presence in her life, offering advice and encouragement. Sarah's life, though filled with moments of brilliance and insight, also had its share of contradictions. She often spoke of the importance of living in alignment with one's values and pursuing one's dreams, but her own choices and actions seemed to veer off course. It was as if Sarah possessed the knowledge and the words but struggled to apply them to her own life.

Kristol wondered if there was a disconnect between the advice Sarah offered and the life she lived. Her best friend's well-intentioned counsel had often led Kristol to question her own path. Was she too caught up in the pursuit of external success, just like everyone else in the office? Or was there something more waiting to be discovered within herself?

As she pondered the possibility of a different life, a voice came from outside the office doorway and interrupted her thoughts. It was her co-worker, Seth, a tall, wiry man with an air of perpetual enthusiasm. His booming voice carried across the office as he engaged in a lively conversation with another colleague.

"Hey, Kristol," Seth greeted her with a warm smile as he strolled over to her office. "Welcome back! It's been way too quiet around here without you. How are you?"

"Thanks, Seth," she replied, trying to muster a sense of enthusiasm. "It's good to be back, I think."

Seth leaned against the edge of her office door, his eyes twinkling with intrigue. "You won't believe the office gossip that's been circulating while you were away. Drama, scandal, and more drama! You've missed out on quite the show."

Kristol couldn't help but chuckle at Seth's animated delivery.

"Fill me in," she said, momentarily forgetting her contemplation of the dream-like world and her internal quest for change.

Seth launched into a whirlwind of stories and anecdotes, sharing the latest office happenings with conviction. He recounted updates on the office romances, rivalries, and quirky incidents that had unfolded during her absence, weaving a narrative that both amused and intrigued Kristol.

As she listened to Seth's stories, Kristol couldn't deny the familiarity of it all. The corporate world, with its office politics and interpersonal dynamics, had a way of drawing people into its tangled web. It was a world where success was often measured by external markers—job titles, promotions, and financial gains—yet it left a void in her soul that she had been struggling to fill.

Amidst the laughter and gossip, a thought began to form in Kristol's mind, sparked by the wisdom of the fortune cookie she had received: *Embrace happiness, for your feelings shape the world you see.* Observing Seth's abundance of enthusiasm, Kristol found herself pondering the deeper meaning of the fortune cookie's message. "Is this what the fortune cookie meant?" she wondered.

As Seth continued to amuse her with tales of office, Kristol continued to wonder if there was more to her life than the confines of the corporate ladder. She felt a growing desire to explore the uncharted territory of her potential, to tap into the inner wisdom she had briefly touched during her accident.

"Hey, Kristol," Seth began with a conspiratorial grin. "Summer's just around the corner. Got any exciting plans?"

Kristol paused for a moment, her thoughts drifting to the dream-like world she had encountered during her accident. The vibrant colors, the tangible emotions, and a sense of possibility still lingered in her memory.

"Actually," she said slowly, "I've been thinking about doing something a little different this summer."

Seth raised an eyebrow, intrigued by Kristol's cryptic response. "Different how?"

A wistful smile touched Kristol's lips. "I'm not entirely sure yet, but I want to make it meaningful. Maybe take some time for self-discovery, explore new horizons, you know?"

Seth nodded. "That sounds like a plan. Sometimes, we all need a change of scenery to reset and find new perspectives."

As they continued their conversation, the topic shifted to the upcoming office barbecue. It was an annual event that brought together colleagues and clients together for a day of relaxation and camaraderie. Seth's eyes lit up as he shared the details.

"You won't believe what we have in store this year," he said, excitement bubbling in his voice. "We're going all out with a Hawaiian luau theme. Grass skirts, leis, tropical drinks—the whole shebang!"

Kristol couldn't help but laugh at Seth's excitement. "It sounds fantastic," she replied, genuinely looking forward to the upcoming gathering. The prospect of a carefree day filled with fun was a welcome diversion from the questions that had been plaguing her.

Seth leaned in closer, his tone conspiratorial once more. "And you won't believe who's taking charge of the barbecue this year – it was announced earlier this morning—none other than Sarah herself!"

Kristol's eyebrows shot up in surprise. "Sarah, the barbecue maestro?" Kristol chuckled. "That's unexpected. Is she planning to transform the office into a tropical paradise too?"

Seth laughed heartily, his eyes crinkling with amusement. "You know Sarah!"

Just then, Sarah, with a beaming smile, bounced over, "Kristol! Did you hear the good news? I am planning the corporate barbecue this summer."

"Sarah, that's fantastic!" Kristol exclaimed, her enthusiasm matching Sarah's.

Sarah's eyes sparkled. "I've got a ton of creative ideas up my sleeve. How about a tropical luau theme with tiki torches, leis, and a live steel drum band? It would transport us all to an island paradise."

With the excitement of the company barbecue planning session filling the air, Sarah buzzed around the office like a whirlwind of energy and enthusiasm. Her mind flooded with creative ideas and logistics, and she couldn't wait to dive into the preparations.

As Sarah continued to bounce from desk to desk, gathering input and ideas from various colleagues, Kristol and Seth returned to their own tasks. Kristol settled back at her desk, her laptop open and a stack of emails awaiting her attention. She knew that while the barbecue planning was exciting, there were still work-related responsibilities that required her focus.

As Kristol read her emails, she couldn't help but feel a sense of appreciation for her friends. The positive energy and camaraderie in the office were felt, and it was moments like these that made her appreciate the work environment even more.

She began to reply to an overloaded inbox of client inquiries, approved project proposals, and scheduled meetings.

As the hours passed, Kristol gradually made her way through her inbox, addressing each email with care. Her phone occasionally chimed with incoming calls, which she answered with a warm and welcoming demeanor. Despite the busy day, she made an effort to connect with clients and provide them with the attention they deserved.

With a sense of accomplishment, Kristol saved her last email, shut down her computer, and gathered her belongings. The familiar routine of the workday had come to an end, leaving Kristol exhausted. She looked forward to returning home, where she could unwind and recharge for the next day with a glass of wine.

She arrived back home with Bella and Max, her furry pups. Their wagging tails and joyful barks greeted her at the door, a welcome distraction from the mounting sense of dread that had settled in her chest from her workday.

Kristol had postponed dealing with the financial aftermath of the car accident for as long as she could. She knew that the moment had arrived to face the reality of the situation, and it filled her with a deep sense of unease. With trembling hands, she gathered the stack of bills that had piled up on her kitchen counter—medical expenses, car repairs, and insurance deductibles. The numbers seemed to taunt her, a reminder of the fragility of her financial situation.

As she meticulously went through each bill, her heart sank further. The costs were astronomical, far beyond what she had anticipated. Her savings account, which had taken years to build, was dwindling at an alarming rate. It was a stark reminder of how quickly financial stability could unravel with unexpected challenges.

Dread and fear settled in like unwelcome guests, their presence weighing down on Kristol's shoulders. She had always prided herself on her ability to manage her finances responsibly, but this unforeseen accident had thrown her carefully constructed plans into disarray. The uncertainty of her financial future lurked above like a dark cloud.

Bella and Max nuzzled against her, offering comfort and solace in their own way as Kristol stroked their fur absentmindedly. They were her source of unconditional love and support that she cherished.

As she continued to review the bills, Kristol's mind drifted back to the dream-like world she had experienced during her accident. The vibrant colors and possibilities of abundance contrasted sharply with the financial constraints and fears that now consumed her. Her mind wandered to the flower petals, where they blackened with fear and became vibrant with happiness. It was as if she had glimpsed a reality where limitations didn't exist.

The paradox between these two worlds gnawed at her. She couldn't help but wonder if there was a connection between the dream-like realm and her current financial struggles. Was there a hidden message or lesson in her accident? Could the potential she had experienced during that fleeting moment be harnessed to overcome her challenges?

While lost in thought, Kristol's phone buzzed, jolting her back to the present. It was a message from Sarah, whose advice often danced on the edge of irony. The message from Sarah read, "Hey Kristol! Just checking in. Hope you had a great first day back at work!"

Kristol sighed; her feelings of vulnerability intensified by Sarah's message.

The evening wore on, and Kristol couldn't escape the relentless anxiety that had taken hold of her. She had always been diligent about her finances, but the accident had shaken her sense of security. The mounting bills and dwindling savings left her feeling trapped and helpless.

With a heavy heart, Kristol knew that she needed to take action. She couldn't allow fear and uncertainty to dictate her future. As she gazed at Bella and Max, their trusting eyes filled with unwavering faith, she made a silent promise to herself. She would find a way to overcome this challenge and rediscover the abundance she had glimpsed in the dream-like realm.

Chapter Four

A CUP OF FRIENDSHIP

The weekend arrived as a welcome reprieve after a long and exhausting week. Kristol and Sarah found themselves nestled in a corner of their favorite coffee shop, a haven of warmth and tranquility amidst the chaos of urban life. The rich aroma of freshly brewed coffee surrounded them, cocooning their conversation in an atmosphere of familiarity.

Kristol couldn't wait any longer to approach the subject that had piqued her interest back at the office earlier in the week. With a steaming mocha in her hands, she asked, "So, Sarah, spill the beans! How did you end up in charge of the company barbecue this year?"

Sarah's eyes twinkled with a mischievous glint; her voice lowered slightly. "Well, you know Kristol, they say it's all about timing and being in the right place at the right time." She took a sip of her cappuccino, savoring the rich blend of flavors before continuing. "I happened to be chatting with Matt Anderson by the coffee machine, and he mentioned that they were looking for someone to organize this year's barbecue. Apparently, the previous organizer had a family emergency and had to step down."

Kristol raised an eyebrow, her curiosity piqued. "And you volunteered just like that?"

Sarah giggled with a hint of self-assuredness in her reply. "Not exactly. I did mention that I had some experience organizing events in my previous job, and I might have suggested a few creative ideas for the barbecue." She winked playfully. "I think my enthusiasm got the better of me."

Kristol couldn't help but smile at her friend's exuberance. Sarah always plunged headfirst into new challenges. "I see," Kristol said, her tone laced with amusement. "So, what's in the grand Hawaiian theme for this year's barbecue?"

Sarah leaned back in her chair, her gaze drifting toward the window where the morning sunlight filtered through the leaves of a nearby tree. "I thought it would be fun to shake things up a bit," she began, her voice filled with joy. "In addition to the traditional grass skirts, leis, and tropical drinks—I thought it would also be fun to roast a pig and have a hula dance contest! A chance for everyone to let loose and forget about the daily grind."

Kristol couldn't help but laugh at Sarah's enthusiasm. The idea of a tropical-themed barbecue sounded like a refreshing change of pace. "That does sound like a lot of fun," she admitted. "But a hula dance contest?" Questioned Kristol. "And remember, organizing such an event can be a lot of work, especially with our busy schedules."

Sarah nodded in agreement. "You're absolutely right, Kristol. It's going to be a bit challenging, but I see it as an opportunity to bring a bit of joy and excitement into the office. Plus, it's a chance to practice what I preach—embracing change and creating memorable experiences."

Kristol admired her friend's unwavering commitment to infuse positivity into every aspect of life. "You've always been good at that, Sarah," she said with genuine appreciation.

Sarah's cheeks flushed with humility as she offered a modest shrug. "I just believe in living life to the fullest and helping others do the same. Sometimes, we all need a little push to break out of our comfort zones, including me."

As they continued their conversation, the topic shifted to the logistics of the upcoming barbecue. Sarah eagerly shared her plans for entertainment and games. Kristol couldn't help but be in the prospect of a memorable day at the office barbecue began to fill her with anticipation.

Sarah, her curly hair cascading like a waterfall of chestnut waves, leaned forward, her eyes filled with delight. "So, Kristol, what's this news you wanted to talk about?"

Kristol hesitated for a moment, her coffee cup cradled in her hands. She had been mulling over her thoughts since the incident, and she wasn't quite sure how to articulate her feelings and aspirations. "Well, Sarah, it's just... I've been doing a lot of soul-searching lately. The accident, it...it shook me. I realized that I've been on this relentless pursuit of success, but it often feels empty, you know?"

Sarah nodded empathetically, sipping her latte. "I get it, Kristol. Sometimes, we get caught up in the rat race, chasing external markers of success, and we forget what truly matters." She placed her cup back on the saucer and leaned forward, her gaze locked onto Kristol's.

Kristol's eyes brightened as she mustered the courage to share her new perspective. "Well," she began, her voice filled with a mixture of anticipation and determination, "I've decided to take some time off this summer. I want to explore new horizons, maybe even discover a different way of living and experiencing life."

Sarah's brown eyes widened with surprise. "That's incredible, Kristol! I mean, it's a bold move, but it sounds like exactly what you need. Have you figured out where you want to go or what you want to do?"

Kristol shook her head, a playful grin dancing on her lips. "Not yet, but that's part of the adventure, right? I want to keep it open-ended and let life surprise me. It's a bit scary, I won't lie, but I think it's time for me to step out of my comfort zone."

Sarah's face lit up with excitement, her voice hushed eagerly. "I love it, Kristol! This choice is exactly what I've been talking about—embracing change, seeking inner wisdom, and chasing your dreams. It's like you're following in my footsteps."

Kristol chuckled, her gaze fixed on her friend's animated expression. "Yes, it's a bit like that, isn't it? But it's also a way for me to explore who I am truly, beyond the corporate world and other people's expectations. I want to tap into the potential I saw after the accident a few weeks ago, that dream-like world. There is something more to life, of that, I am certain."

Sarah was understanding. "I believe in you, Kristol. You have the courage and the heart to make this journey meaningful and transformative. And hey, I'll be cheering you on every step of the way."

As the conversation continued, Kristol found herself compelled to share the vivid details of the dream-like world that had been haunting her thoughts since the car accident. She described the contrast between that otherworldly realm and the mundane routines of her corporate job.

"It's as if I stepped into a different reality, between the car crash and the hospital," Kristol began, her voice tinged with wonder. "The colors were so vibrant, Sarah, more vivid than anything I've ever seen. Emotions were real, and the flowers responded to how I felt."

Sarah's eyes widened with apprehension as she said, "I'm not sure, Kristol. It sounds interesting, but I'm a bit worried."

Kristol's eyes were far off in the distance with the memory of the dream-like world. "In that realm or dimension, whatever it was, I felt an overwhelming sense of abundance and possibility. The world around me transformed, time warping my senses, and suddenly, everything blended together. There was no fear, no scarcity, just an immense feeling of being connected to something greater."

Sarah attentively listened.

"But when fear arose, everything around me responded," Kristol continued, "as if my existence trembled in its presence. The flowers recoiled and withered, turning black. It was as though the universe whispered caution in my ear, urging me to tread carefully on the path ahead."

Sarah raised an eyebrow, glancing at Kristol, reacting questionably.

"You know, Sarah," Kristol continued, "it's strange how this dream-like world contrasts with the reality of my everyday life. I've been chasing success and recognition in my career, just like everyone else in the office. But it often feels empty, like I'm on a never-ending treadmill."

Kristol hesitated, knowing that her next words might challenge the authenticity of her friend's guidance. "It's just that, well, you've always encouraged me to seek change and pursue my dreams and financial success. But sometimes, I wonder if you're also caught in that same pursuit. Your advice is so inspiring, yet I've seen how your own choices and actions seem to veer off course."

Sarah's expression shifted, the vulnerability in her eyes mixed with annoyance at being called out. She didn't seem surprised by Kristol's observation. "You're right, Kristol. I've had my own struggles and contradictions," she admitted, her voice defensive. "It's not always easy to live in alignment with your values and pursue your dreams."

Quickly, Sarah composed herself, taking a deep breath before continuing with a more even tone, "It's just that sometimes life throws curveballs, you know? We find ourselves making compromises and taking detours. But that doesn't mean we've abandoned our core beliefs. It means we're adapting to the circumstances."

Kristol reached out and placed her hand over Sarah's, a gesture of understanding. "I know you do, Sarah, and that's why I value your advice so much. It's just that, as I explore, I want to ensure that I'm following a path that's authentic to me, one that is in alignment – like that other world place I was in after the accident.

When the tension diffused, Sarah shifted the conversation back to the Hawaiian luau-themed barbecue, a topic that had initially brought them together for coffee. "Speaking of our office luau, Kristol," Sarah began, her voice animated, "With all this talk about flowers, what if we took a little detour into the flower district to handpick the most exquisite tropical flowers for the barbecue?"

Kristol's eyes widened at Sarah's suggestion. The thought of venturing into the heart of the flower district seemed like an opportunity for the potential answers.

"That sounds incredible, Sarah," Kristol exclaimed, her exuberance matching her friend's. She couldn't help but smile at this impromptu adventure. "I'm definitely on board."

Sarah clapped her hands together, her face lit up with delight. "I knew you'd be up for it!"

Finishing their coffee, Kristol nodded in agreement, feeling a renewed sense of purpose. Kristol appreciated the spontaneity of the moment. She had spent so long immersed in the routines and demands of her corporate job until the car accident that she had forgotten the thrill of unexpected adventures.

The transition from the quiet coffee shop to the crowded streets was almost unbearable. The city's relentless energy seemed to converge in this neighborhood. They arrived at the flower district, where an array of flowers and plants spilled onto the sidewalks in a riot of colors and scents.

The district was alive with nature's beauty, a place where reality intertwined with the extraordinary. Rows of stalls and shops lined the streets, their dynamic displays capturing the essence of a tropical paradise. Exotic blooms, lush foliage, and fragrant blossoms competed for attention, creating a captivating experience that surrounded Kristol and Sarah in its embrace.

Kristol, aided by her crutches, moved through the district with a sense of determination and wonder. She was amazed by the sheer diversity of the flowers and the vibrant atmosphere of the place.

"Isn't this place amazing, Kristol?" Sarah exclaimed.

"It's incredible," Kristol agreed, her voice tinged with awe. "Her gaze wandered over the rows of flowers. "I never imagined there was a place like this in the middle of the city."

As they continued exploring the different flower stands, Sarah initiated a friendly competition to see who could spot the most exotic blooms. They laughed and marveled at the unique varieties they discovered, from orchids with intricate patterns to towering sunflowers with golden crowns.

Kristol felt carefree and liberated in this vibrant environment. She inhaled deeply, savoring the rich, earthy scents that surrounded her. The flower district reminded her of the dream-like world she experienced after the car crash.

"Hey, Kristol," Sarah called out from a nearby flower stall, her voice filled with excitement. "Come over here! I think I've found the perfect centerpiece for our luau."

Kristol walked over in her crutches; her curiosity piqued. Sarah was admiring a stunning arrangement of tropical flowers in vibrant shades of pink, orange, and purple. The centerpiece exuded an air of tropical extravagance, and Kristol couldn't help but be captivated by its beauty.

"That's absolutely gorgeous," Kristol exclaimed, her eyes fixed on the arrangement. "It's like a burst of paradise." Sarah agrees and decides to place the order for the Hawaiian barbeque.

Kristol, wandering off, came across a small, tucked-away flower shop that seemed to emit an air of enchantment. The shop was adorned with hanging baskets overflowing with vibrant flowers, and the scent of exotic flowers wafted from within.

Kristol felt drawn to the shop's entrance. She glanced at Sarah, who was engrossed in selecting the final blooms for their luau arrangement. With a quick nod to her friend, Kristol stepped into the flower shop.

The interior was a botanical wonderland. Countless varieties of flowers and plants filled every available space, creating a lush tapestry of colors and scents. The shop was bathed in the warm, diffused light that filtered through the leaves, casting a magical glow over everything.

As Kristol gazed at the flowers, she couldn't help but feel that everything around her was vibrating at a higher frequency. It was as though time itself had lost its significance in this mesmerizing moment.

She was admiring a display of exotic orchids when a soft, melodious voice caught her attention. Turning, she saw an elderly woman with a kind, weathered face and twinkling eyes. The woman was tending to a collection of bonsai trees with loving care.

"Beautiful, aren't they?" the woman said, her voice as soothing as a gentle breeze. "Each one tells a story, you know. They have a way of capturing the essence of life."

Kristol nodded. "They're incredible. I've always been fascinated by bonsai trees."

The woman smiled warmly. "Ah, a kindred spirit, I see. Bonsai trees teach us patience, resilience, and the art of embracing imperfections. They remind us that growth is a lifelong journey."

Kristol found herself drawn to the woman's wisdom and the sense of calm that seemed to emanate from her. It was as if the flower shop itself held secrets waiting to be discovered.

"I'm Isabella," the woman introduced herself, extending a hand. "But you can call me Isa. I've tended to these trees for as long as I can remember."

Kristol shook Isa's hand, feeling an instant connection. "I'm Kristol. It's a pleasure to meet you, Isa."

Isa's eyes twinkled with amusement. "Kristol, I sense a spirit of adventure in you, a longing for something. Am I right?"

Kristol was taken aback by the accuracy of Isa's words. It was as if the woman had peered into her soul and recognized the yearning she had been grappling with.

"You're perceptive," Kristol admitted, intrigued. "Lately, I've been feeling like there's more to life than what I've known."

Isa nodded knowingly. "Life has a way of leading us down unexpected paths, revealing hidden treasures along the way. Sometimes, all it takes is a single step in a new direction."

As Kristol absorbed Isa's words, she felt a gentle tug at her heart—a call to embrace the sense of adventure that had been simmering within her. It was an invitation to explore and discover a parallel life in the present day.

"Isa, do you ever feel like there's a world beyond what we see with our eyes?" Kristol asked, her voice filled with curiosity.

Isa's smile deepened, and she nodded. "Oh, my dear, there are worlds within worlds waiting to be explored. Emotions, thoughts, and feelings—they hold the key to unlocking the extraordinary within the ordinary."

Kristol's thoughts raced with fascination. She had glimpsed a taste of this extraordinary world during her accident, and now, in this flower shop.

"It's a realm where thoughts share reality," Isa continued. "All you have to do is walk through the threshold of those arching trees. "Isa nodded towards the trees.

Kristol's heart fluttered. The invitation Isa presented was undeniably fascinating, but it also stirred deep-seated apprehension within her. She appreciated the offer, but the idea of crossing that threshold felt daunting.

Kristol's voice quivered with uncertainty. "I appreciate your invitation, Isa, but I need to get back to my friend," she shared, the words tumbling out as she felt a rush of anxiety. With a quick nod and a hurried "thank you," Kristol hastily left the flower stand, her heart pounding.

Isa's words lingered in Kristol's mind as she rejoined Sarah amid the vibrant blooms. The allure of the extraordinary world, the dream-like realm, tugged at her heartstrings like a siren's call.

As she walked alongside Sarah, crutches in hand, her mind was a whirlwind of thoughts and possibilities. Kristol couldn't help but wonder what lay beyond the arching trees Isa had mentioned.

Sarah noticed the far-off look in Kristol's eyes and nudged her playfully. "Earth to Kristol! You've been in la-la land for a while. What's going on in that brilliant mind of yours?"

Kristol hesitated, torn between the pull of curiosity and the grip of fear. "Sarah, do you ever feel like there's a world beyond what we see with our eyes?"

Sarah raised an eyebrow, intrigued by Kristol's question. "You mean like another dimension or something?"

Kristol nodded, her voice tinged with uncertainty. "Yeah, something like that. Isa, the woman in the flower shop, mentioned it too. She talked about emotions, thoughts, and feelings holding the key to unlocking the extraordinary within the ordinary."

Sarah chuckled, though her eyes held a glint of intrigue. "That sounds like something out of a sci-fi movie, Kris. Are you thinking about becoming a psychic or something?"

Kristol couldn't help but laugh at Sarah's playful skepticism. "No, it's not about becoming a psychic. It's more about exploring the depths of our own mind, I think, and understanding the power of our thoughts and emotions."

Sarah shrugged, "Well, it's an interesting concept, for sure. But we live in the real world, Kris, with bills to pay, jobs to attend to, and responsibilities to fulfill. Sometimes, we have to keep our feet on the ground."

Kristol knew that Sarah had a point. The practical demands of their everyday lives couldn't be ignored. Yet, Isa's invitation continued to echo in her heart.

Chapter Five

CROSSROADS OF REFLECTION

Kristol found herself back in the rhythm of her everyday life back home after leaving the flower district. The encounter with Isa remained in her thoughts, but the demands of her corporate job and the mounting bills still pressed upon her. She decided to take a break from her financial worries and headed to the nearby park to enjoy some sunshine with her pups.

As Kristol strolled along the winding path, the rustling leaves and the gentle breeze offered comfort, providing a brief break from the chaos of her mind. It was during this peaceful walk that she encountered Liam, a familiar face in the park. Liam was a kind-hearted man with a fondness for striking up conversations with fellow park-goers. He had a warm smile and a demeanor that put people at ease.

Kristol returned his smile, grateful for the friendly interruption to her thoughts. "Hi, Liam. How's it going?" Their dogs wasted no time in joining forces for a spirited game of chase and tag. Max's boundless energy was contagious, and even Bella, known for her more reserved nature, couldn't resist the urge to join in the fun with Liam's pup.

As the dogs playfully raced around, Liam turned his attention to Kristol, his eyes glancing down at her leg, which was no longer encumbered by crutches. "I see your leg's healing up nicely," he remarked.

Kristol nodded, a grateful smile on her lips. "Yes, it's coming along well."

As they walked together, Liam sensed that something weighed on Kristol's mind. "You seem a bit preoccupied today, Kristol. Anything on your mind that you'd like to share?"

Kristol hesitated for a moment, unsure if she should open up to Liam about the strange encounter at the flower shop and the invitation from Isa. But there was something about his presence that made her feel safe as if he could see through the layers of her facade.

"Well," she began, "I had this…strange experience at a flower district last week. I met someone named Isa, and she invited me to walk through some trees to explore something different, where thoughts share reality. I am really confused by this, but since the accident, nothing makes much sense anymore."

Liam listened attentively. He had an uncanny ability to make people feel heard and understood. "That does sound interesting," he replied, "Tell me more."

Kristol shared more of the details of her visit to the flower shop, the vivid colors, and the emotional connection she had experienced. She talked more about Isa's invitation to enter a world that seemed to hold the key to her innermost desires and the lessons she had learned from her accident.

Liam nodded thoughtfully, his eyes reflecting the wisdom of someone who had seen their fair share of life's ups and downs. "It sounds like a synchronistic encounter, Kristol. Sometimes, the most unexpected experiences can hold the keys to our deepest desires and the answers to our questions."

Kristol couldn't help but feel a sense of comfort in Liam's words. He continued, "Sometimes, we find ourselves at a crossroads, unsure of which path to take. But remember, Kristol, the heart knows the way. When you listen to your heart and follow what truly resonates with your soul, you'll find the path that leads to your deepest fulfillment."

His words resonated with Kristol, who had been grappling with questions about her career, her values, and her pursuit of success. The encounter at the flower shop and her conversation with Liam seemed to be nudging her in a direction she hadn't considered before—a direction that aligned with the desires of her heart.

Kristol took a deep breath and looked out at the serene surroundings. The lush greenery and the gentle sway of the trees seemed to echo Liam's words, reminding her that there was more to life than the corporate ladder and the pursuit of success. "Thank you, Liam," she said, her voice filled with gratitude. "Your words mean a lot to me. It's just...sometimes, it's hard to break free from the expectations and pressures of the world."

As Kristol and Liam continued their leisurely stroll through the park, the sun cast a warm, golden hue over the tranquil surroundings.

"So, Liam," Kristol began, breaking the comfortable silence that had settled between them, "What has been happening in your life?"

Liam smiled warmly, his eyes reflecting a sense of contentment. "Well, Kristol," he began, "I began working as a marketing consultant for a tech company a few weeks ago. It's a demanding job, but I enjoy the challenges it brings."

Kristol nodded. "Starting a new job can be both exciting and overwhelming. I hope you find it fulfilling and rewarding."

Liam chuckled lightly. "I'm still getting my bearings and learning the ropes. It's been quite a whirlwind, but I'm enjoying it." He continued, "I've always been fascinated by the tech industry, and this opportunity feels like a perfect fit for me."

Kristol smiled, sensing Liam's genuine passion for his new role. "That's wonderful to hear. It's always inspiring to meet someone so enthusiastic about their work. And what about your life outside of work? What have you been doing for fun?"

Liam's expression lit up as he shared his interests. "Absolutely! I'm an avid hiker and love spending weekends exploring the nearby trails and canyons. Nature has this incredible way of rejuvenating the spirit, don't you think?"

They continued walking, their conversation weaving effortlessly between topics of work, hobbies, and life in the city. The more they talked, the more Kristol felt a sense of familiarity and connection with Liam, as if they were old friends catching up after a long absence.

As the conversation with Liam came to a close, Kristol was left alone with her thoughts. She couldn't help but ponder the connection between what Liam shared and the invitation from Isa to explore a parallel world at the flower shop. The idea both intrigued and unsettled her. Was it a path worth pursuing, or was it simply a fleeting curiosity?

Kristol needed to find out, but she knew that she needed time to process her thoughts and feelings. The financial pressures and the demands of her corporate job still loomed in the back of her mind, but Liam's words had planted a seed of possibility. She realized that there was more to life than the relentless pursuit of success and recognition.

As Kristol was leaving the park, the scent of freshly cut grass and the distant laughter of children lingered in the air. As she drove back home, her thoughts drifted back to her conversation with Liam.

Arriving at her condo, Kristol parked her car and made her way inside with Bella and Max, exhausted from their park adventure. Kristol started cooking dinner, picked up her phone to call Sarah, and noticed a missed call from her mother. Evelyn had been checking on Kristol regularly since the accident.

Kristol dialed her mother's number and waited as it rang. After a few moments, Evelyn's voice filled the line. "Kristol, how are you doing today?"

"I'm doing better, Mom," Kristol replied, a hint of fatigue in her voice. "The doctor says my leg is healing well, and soon I can have this brace off."

Evelyn's relief was evident. "That is wonderful news! I worry about you so much. How's your spirit holding up?"

Kristol hesitated for a moment, contemplating how to express her feelings. Liam's words about the power of perception and emotion still echoed in her mind. She considered confiding in her mother, sharing her encounter with the flower shop she had recently undergone. However, a sense of uncertainty held her back. Instead, she decided to keep this new chapter of her life to herself for the time being, unsure of how it would be received.

"Mom, my spirit is fine," Kristol replied, deflecting the question about her emotional well-being. She wanted to keep the conversation light and avoid delving into the complexities of her recent experiences.

Evelyn, sensing her daughter's hesitation, chose not to press further. Instead, she shifted the conversation to a more casual tone. "That's good to hear, dear. How about we plan a nice dinner together next weekend? I'd love to catch up."

Kristol appreciated her mother's offer but had to decline. "I would love that, Mom, but I have a work barbecue planned for next weekend. It's an important event, and I'll be quite busy with preparations."

Evelyn understood the demands of Kristol's career and nodded understandingly. "Of course. Your career is important, and

I'm proud of all you've achieved. We'll plan that dinner for another time when your schedule permits." Her mother said, disappointed.

After her conversation with her mother, Kristol hung up the phone and returned to her kitchen, where the aroma of a homemade dinner filled the air. She decided to prepare a comforting meal, something that would soothe her senses and help her unwind from the day's events.

As she moved around the kitchen, chopping vegetables and seasoning the dishes, Kristol couldn't help but reflect on the recent turn of events in her life and what it all meant. Kristol felt a deep connection to the vibrant, magical world tugging at her heartstrings, urging her to explore further.

As Kristol ate her dinner, she found herself in a contemplative mood. She knew she should call Sarah and share her plans for returning to the flower district, but something held her back. As Kristol cleaned up the dishes, she glanced at her phone, hesitating for a moment. The movie she had wanted to watch had already started playing on the TV, and it seemed like a perfect distraction from the thoughts swirling in her mind. With a sigh, she decided to indulge in the comedy while a sense of guilt washed over her.

Kristol settled onto the sofa, propping her feet up on the coffee table. The movie played on the screen, its plot slowly drawing her in. The characters, their stories, and the world they inhabited began to capture her attention. As the movie unfolded, Kristol found herself engrossed in its narrative, her mind momentarily free from the weight of her recent experiences. She tried to focus on the storyline, allowing the cinematic world to take her away from her own thoughts and concerns.

But as the minutes ticked by and the movie continued, Kristol became restless. Kristol glanced at her phone once more, contemplating whether to reach out to Sarah and share her intentions to return to the flower district. She knew that a simple call could ease her friend's worries and provide a sense of clarity.

With a deep breath, Kristol decided to put off the call to Sarah for now. She settled back into the sofa, fully immersing herself in the humor and laughter that the movie provided. Kristol soon found herself chuckling at the witty dialogue and comedic situations it presented.

As the time passed, Kristol's eyes began to grow heavy. The comfort of her living room and the lightheartedness of the movie lulled her into a sense of relaxation with Max and Bella curled up by her side, adding to the warmth and peace of the moment.

Kristol dozed off. In her sleep, Kristol's mind continued to drift and dream of the unknown world.

Chapter Six

A LEAP OF FAITH

The following day, Kristol found herself standing before the arching trees that marked the entrance to the pathway at Isa's flower stand. The tantalizing possibility of another world beyond those trees had continually permeated her thoughts. Sarah's words echoed in her mind, reminding her of the responsibilities and practicalities of their lives. It was easy to get swept away by the allure of a different reality.

It was a leap of faith, a step into the unknown, that she couldn't deny any longer. The monotony of her daily routine felt suffocating, and she found herself yearning for a taste of something different. Liam's words from their encounter in the park, his encouragement to follow her heart and embrace the unknown, resonated deeply inside her.

Her heart raced; her palms grew sweaty. Fear still gnawed at the edges of her mind, but she refused to let it hold her back any longer. Isa's words echoed in her memory: "All you have to do is walk through the trees, Kristol. Trust your instincts."

With a deep breath, Kristol braced herself and took that first step, walking under the arching trees. The world around her seemed to shift and shimmer, and a sense of weightlessness washed over her. The familiar surroundings of the flower district transformed into something altogether different. She found herself surrounded by an ethereal landscape where vibrant colors danced in harmony with the gentle whispers of the soft breeze.

Flowers of every imaginable hue stretched toward the sky, their petals soft to the touch. The air was filled with the sweet scent of honey, a fragrance that reminded her of childhood. Feelings of bliss and euphoria swept through her, filling the air around her with an abundant energy of joy and happiness.

With each step she took, Kristol felt a profound shift within herself. The restlessness that had plagued her had dissipated, replaced by a sense of belonging and purpose. It was as though she had finally found her place in a world that resonated with the deepest recesses of her soul.

As Kristol ventured in deeper, she couldn't help but feel a profound sense of peace and contentment. Kristol's senses were alive with wonder; she suddenly felt a presence beside her. Startled, she turned around, her heart pounding, to see an older woman standing there, a twinkle in her eye and a warm smile on her lips.

"I have been waiting for you," the woman said, her voice a soothing melody that seemed to resonate with Kristol.

Kristol blinked in surprise, her mind racing to comprehend the sudden appearance of this stranger. She had not seen anyone else until now, and the woman's presence was unexpected.

The woman extended a hand, jingling with colorful bangle bracelets and rings with every movement. "I am Citta," she introduced herself, her eyes crinkling with amusement. "You must be Kristol, the one who has been called to this place."

Kristol hesitated, her instincts startled. There was something about Citta's presence that felt familiar, safe, and nurturing. With a mixture of apprehension and trust, she reached out cautiously and shook the woman's hand.

"Yes, I'm Kristol," she replied, her voice tinged with a mixture of uncertainty and fascination. "How did you know I would be here? How do you know my name? Kristol questioned.

Citta chuckled softly, her laughter like tinkling wind chimes. "Oh, my dear, time and space are not what they seem. I have been here for as long as I can remember, and I have a way of sensing when someone is ready."

Kristol couldn't help but be captivated by Citta's presence and her beautiful olive skin tone. There was an aura of serenity and knowledge that surrounded her like a living oracle. She gestured toward the breathtaking surroundings. "This place is incredible."

Citta nodded, her gaze sweeping over the vibrant flowers and the ethereal landscape. "It is a place where reality and illusion combine. Here, the wisdom of inner understanding alters time and space, and everything becomes limitless."

As they walked together, Citta shared snippets of wisdom that resonated deeply with Kristol. "You see, the energy of this inner world is different from the one you know. Here, intentions and emotions have the power to shape reality. What you feel and believe becomes your truth."

Kristol listened attentively, her heart open to the teachings of this wise stranger. Citta's words seemed to unlock something within her, an unexpected inner-connectedness.

"Life in the ordinary world," Citta continued, "often leads us to forget the magic that resides within us. We become ensnared by fears and doubts, limiting ourselves. But here, you have the opportunity to rediscover your true essence and harness the energy of creation."

Kristol turned to Citta, "Citta, I'm fascinated by what you're saying," her brow furrowed slightly, "but I am also confused by what you are saying. How exactly do intentions and emotions shape reality here? And what do you mean by rediscovering our true essence? It all sounds amazing, but I don't understand what you mean."

Citta, seemingly ignoring Kristol's question, was grinning.

"You won't believe what happened to me the other day, Kristol! I was in the grocery store, just minding my own business, when I found myself in the cereal aisle. Now, I don't know about you, but I find cereal shopping to be a daunting task. There are just too many options, right?"

Kristol was laughing sarcastically, "Oh, I can relate to that! It's like choosing a cereal is a life-altering decision."

"Exactly!" Citta said. "So, there I am, staring at the endless boxes of cereal, trying to figure out which one to pick. And then, it happened. I saw a box with a picture of a happy family on it, all smiles and sunshine. And guess what it said? 'Start your day with happiness and rainbows!' Can you believe it?"

"Happiness and rainbows? In a cereal box? That's a bit optimistic, isn't it?" Kristol replied, wondering where all of this was going.

"Oh, it gets better! I thought, 'Why not give it a try?' So, I grabbed that box and headed to the checkout counter, feeling like I was about to embark on a magical cereal adventure." Responded Citta.

Kristol asked, "And did you?" curiously.

"Oh, you bet I did! I got home, poured myself a bowl of that 'happiness and rainbows' cereal, and took a big bite. But you know what happened next?"

Kristol was curious. "What happened?"

Overly dramatic, Citta replied, "It tasted like cardboard with a hint of disappointment! I mean, seriously, where were the rainbows, Kristol? Where was the happiness?"

Kristol, uncontrollably laughing, "I guess you can't always find happiness in a cereal box."

"Exactly! And that's when it hit me." Exclaimed Citta. "Life in the ordinary world is a lot like that cereal aisle. We're bombarded with all these promises of happiness and rainbows, but sometimes, we end up with cardboard and disappointment. So, I decided to stick to what I know best—creating my own happiness and rainbows, one joke at a time!"

Kristol was smiling and unable to contain herself. "Citta, what is your secret recipe for happiness and rainbows?"

Citta winked. "Well, it all starts with a good laugh and a hearty dose of humor. You see, Kristol, happiness isn't something you find outside of yourself; it's a treasure that resides within. Laughter is the real magic, the key to unlocking that inner joy. It can turn any ordinary moment into something extraordinary."

Kristol furrowed her brow, still processing Citta's words. "But, Citta, how can something as simple as laughter and humor unlock happiness that's supposedly inside us? I mean, isn't happiness about external circumstances, like achieving our goals or having the right things in life?"

Citta chuckled softly and patted Kristol's shoulder. "Ah, you've touched upon a common misconception. The truth is, the external world can offer fleeting moments of joy, but it's like chasing rainbows in the sky—you might catch a glimpse, but they'll always remain just out of reach."

Kristol pondered Citta's words. "So, you're saying that happiness is something we already have within us, but we've just forgotten how to access it?"

Citta nodded, her eyes filled with wisdom. "Precisely! Life in the ordinary world often leads us to forget the magic that resides within us. We become ensnared by fears and doubts, limiting ourselves. We forget that we are the creators of our own reality, and our thoughts and emotions shape the world around us."

Kristol's curiosity deepened. "But how do we break free from those limitations and rediscover our true essence?"

Citta gestured to the world around them, the vibrant flowers and the bustling energy of the flower district. "By embracing the energy of creation. What you feel and believe becomes your truth. When you infuse your thoughts with humor, when you can laugh at life's absurdities, you dismantle those self-imposed limitations. You reconnect with the limitless possibilities of existence."

Citta continued, "Embrace happiness, for your feelings shape the world you see." nodding towards a sign that went unnoticed by Kristol.

Kristol, looking intently and trying to grasp what Citta was saying, furrowed her brow in confusion. Her mind churned as she contemplated the meaning behind those words. She had experienced moments of happiness, and she had felt the impact of her emotions, but she couldn't quite fathom how they shaped the world around her.

Citta, with her peaceful demeanor, seemed to sense Kristol's confusion. She gently reached out and touched Kristol's hand. "I know it might sound a bit abstract, but let me break it down for you," Citta began, her eyes kind and understanding.

"Imagine that your feelings are like a brushstroke on the canvas of your life. Each emotion you experience is like a color, and every thought is a stroke. When you embrace happiness and let it flow through you, it's as if you're painting your world with vibrant and joyful hues. Your reality becomes a masterpiece filled with beauty and magic."

Kristol's gaze shifted to the sign that Citta had pointed out earlier. It was a simple wooden board with those very words inscribed in elegant script: "Embrace happiness, for your feelings shape the world you see."

Citta continued, "Now when you dwell in fear, doubt, or negativity, it's like using dark and somber colors on your canvas. Your world takes on a different tone, one that is less inviting and less vibrant."

Then it clicked. The fortune cookie that Kristol received after returning home from the hospital had the same saying. "I see it now," Kristol murmured, her eyes returning to meet Citta's. "It's like a dance between my feelings and the world. When I'm happy, the world becomes a happier place."

Citta smiled warmly, pleased with Kristol's growing understanding. "Exactly. Your emotions are like a tuning fork that resonates with the universe. When you vibrate with happiness, you attract more of it into your life."

Kristol couldn't help but dig deeper. "Citta, I understand that happiness is on the inside, and it connects us to all possibilities. But what about the practical aspects of life, like finances, money, and abundance? How does this concept translate into real-world success?"

Citta's gaze held a hint of mystery as she responded, "Ah, Kristol, the journey to discovering the magic within and the pursuit of abundance in the ordinary world are intertwined. When you align your inner happiness with your external desires, you create a powerful synergy."

Kristol, eager to grasp the wisdom Citta was sharing, said, "But how does that synergy work? Can you give me an example?"

Before Citta could reply, a sudden gust of wind rustled through the trees, and the flower district seemed to shimmer momentarily. Kristol blinked in surprise, and when she looked back to where Citta had stood, the enigmatic woman was gone.

In her place, a whisper carried by the wind reached Kristol's ears. "Trust in happiness. It will guide you on your path."

Kristol scanned the surroundings, but there was no sign of Citta. She was left with more questions than answers, pondering the mysterious connection between inner happiness, external success, and the infinite possibilities that lay ahead.

As Kristol turned to leave the flower stand, her gaze met Isa's, who was tending to a colorful display of orchids. Isa's eyes held a depth of understanding that resonated with Kristol. Without exchanging words, Kristol offered a nod of gratitude, silently acknowledging the guidance she had received. Isa smiled warmly in return, a silent reassurance that she would be here whenever Kristol was ready to return to the other world. With that unspoken connection, Kristol continued on her path, her heart a little lighter and her mind filled with many more questions and uncertainty.

Chapter Seven

BALANCING ACT

Monday morning arrived, and as Kristol walked into the corporate office, a subtle but significant shift had occurred within her. She no longer viewed her role in the same light. However, the gnawing feeling that she was trading her time for money was in the back of her mind.

As she settled in her office, Seth greeted her with a smile. "Morning, Kristol!" Seth chirped. "How was your weekend? Do anything exciting?"

Kristol hesitated for a moment, her mind still dwelling on the experiences of the flower shop. "You know, Seth," she began, "I did something different this weekend. I had this realization that there's more to life than just the daily grind. I mean, why are we trading our time for money?"

Seth leaned in, intrigued by Kristol's change in perspective. "That's an interesting question," he said. "I mean, work is necessary, right? We need to pay the bills and all that."

Kristol nodded thoughtfully. "Of course, I get that. But what if there's a way to align our work with our passions, to do something that truly fulfills us and brings meaning to our lives?"

Seth raised an eyebrow. "Are you suggesting that we all quit our jobs and pursue our wildest dreams?"

Kristol chuckled. "Not exactly, but I think we can find a balance. Maybe we can explore what truly makes us happy and see how we can integrate it into our lives, even within the confines of our jobs."

Seth considered her words. "I guess it's about finding purpose and fulfillment in what we do, right?"

"Exactly," Kristol replied. "And maybe, just maybe, there's more to life than the office."

Kristol and Seth were suddenly interrupted by Sarah's energetic entrance. She burst into the office with a stack of colorful flyers in her hand, her enthusiasm for the Hawaiian luau reaching new heights.

Excitedly, Sarah exclaimed, "Aloha, my fellow party barbecue people! I've got the official luau flyers hot off the press!"

Kristol and Seth exchanged amusing glances as Sarah practically danced into the room.

Teasingly, Kristol laughs, "Sarah, you're like a walking luau advertisement. Are you sure you're not secretly moonlighting as a hula dancer?"

"Oh, wouldn't that be a hoot?" mused Sarah. "But no, my talents are reserved for event planning and luau promotion."

Seth was grinning, "Well, you're doing an excellent job at it. I'm getting more excited about this luau by the second."

"That's the spirit, Seth!" said Sarah, waving the flyers, "And you haven't seen anything yet. Wait till you see the decorations we have in store. It's going to be like stepping into the tropical paradise of Hawaii!"

Kristol couldn't help but admire Sarah's dedication to making the Hawaiian luau a memorable event. It was clear that she wanted everyone to have a fantastic time.

"Sarah, you've been buzzing around like a busy bee, and I have to admit, I'm starting to get caught up in the luau fever. What's the big surprise you've been teasing us about?" asked Kristol.

"Ah, Kristol, I can't spill all the coconuts just yet." Said Sarah mysteriously, "But let's just say there's a special performance in the works that will blow everyone away. It's going to be a luau like no other!"

Seth was intrigued, "A special performance? You've got our attention, Sarah."

Mischievously, Sarah said, "Oh, you'll have to wait and see. It's a surprise that's going to make waves, I promise."

Kristol couldn't help but be swept up in the excitement. Sarah's passion for the luau was undeniable, and it was starting to feel like a welcome diversion from her recent contemplations about life's purpose.

Kristol was smiling, "Well, I'm looking forward to it, Sarah. And if you need any help with the flower arrangements or any other preparations, just let me know."

"Thank you, Kristol!" Sarah gratefully said, "Your expertise will make a world of difference."

"Sarah's energy is infectious, isn't it?" Seth smiled. "I can't remember the last time I was this excited about an office event."

Kristol nodded, "She certainly knows how to bring a touch of magic. It's refreshing."

Thoughtfully, Seth brought back the earlier conversation. "You know, Kristol, maybe we've been approaching our jobs the wrong way. We often focus on our careers and routine, but what if we started looking for ways to infuse our work with purpose and fulfillment, just like you said?"

"If happiness is on the inside," Kristol continued, "why do we look outside of ourselves?"

"You raise a good point, Kristol." Seth thought out loud. "It's easy to fall into the trap of seeking happiness externally, whether it's through our jobs, possessions, or even other people. But maybe it's because we've been conditioned to believe that these external factors hold the key to our happiness."

As Kristol was engrossed in her conversation with Seth, her phone suddenly buzzed insistently. Startled, she glanced at the caller ID, revealing a number. Her heart sank as she realized it was from a creditor about a late payment. With a sigh, she quickly silenced the call, but the wave of despair that washed over her was undeniable.

Gathering her composure, Kristol forced a smile and returned her focus to Seth. Despite the financial stress that had momentarily sidetracked her, she continued to carry on with their conversation.

"I think you're right, Seth. Society often promotes the idea that success, wealth, and recognition are the pathways to happiness. But what if the real journey is within ourselves." Kristol engaged.

Seth reflected, "So, what do you think is the key to unlocking that inner happiness, Kristol?"

Kristol's uncertainty hung in the air as she searched for answers within herself.

Apprehensive, "You know, Seth, as much as I believe in the idea of inner happiness, I'm not entirely sure what it looks like for me. It's like trying to find a hidden treasure without a map."

With their conversation coming to a close, Seth and Kristol exchanged smiles before returning to their respective workspaces.

Slowly, the day moved on as if time stood still. Kristol's role as a corporate trainer required her to wear many hats, and today, she had to review the financial reports. As she sat in her office, reviewing spreadsheets and examining budgets, she couldn't help but feel a growing sense of unease.

The numbers on the screen seemed to mock her, whispering doubts and insecurities into her ear. The annual budget, the projections, the balance sheets—they all swirled around her, transforming into a daunting labyrinth that threatened to swallow her up. Fear lurked in the background, ready to pounce on any sign of weakness.

Kristol had always been competent with numbers; her financial ability to make accurate and quick decisions was a source of pride. But today was different. Today, the fear of not measuring up, of making a costly mistake, of financial instability gripped her heart like a vise. It was as if this relentless fear was slowly swallowing the happiness within her.

She glanced at her calendar, where a meeting with her team was scheduled that afternoon. The topic was budget reviews, and she couldn't help but dread it. How could she guide her team when she felt lost in this maze of numbers and fear?

Fear had indeed crept into her heart, casting doubt. She couldn't help but wonder how she could navigate this new challenge on her journey to inner happiness. In these moments, Kristol recognized that fear was the force that had the power to cloud her judgment, steal her happiness, and limit her abundance.

Kristol's phone continued to buzz relentlessly, each call from a different creditor. Overwhelmed by the incessant reminders of her financial troubles, she couldn't bring herself to answer any of them. In a desperate attempt to silence the relentless calls, she eventually turned off her phone.

A wave of inner turmoil washed over her. Her stomach churned with anxiety, and she felt physically sick from the stress of her financial situation. It was a painful reminder of the challenges she faced, and she couldn't help but feel trapped in a seemingly endless cycle of debt and worry.

Kristol entered the sleek and modern conference room on the top floor of the office building. Her team was already gathered around the long table, each member immersed in their laptops and spreadsheets. The room was adorned with floor-to-ceiling windows that offered a panoramic view of the city skyline, but the team's attention was firmly fixed on the task at hand.

"Good afternoon, everyone," Kristol greeted, her voice carrying a blend of authority and warmth. She took her seat at the head of the table, a large screen at the opposite end waiting to display their financial reports.

Her team consisted of dedicated individuals, each with their own area of expertise in financial analysis, forecasting, and budgeting. There was Michael, the meticulous data analyst with a knack for uncovering hidden trends, and Susan, a vibrant and detail-oriented financial planner. Next to them sat Mark, a senior financial analyst known for his calm demeanor under pressure, and Lisa, a rising star in the finance department with a talent for presenting complex data clearly and concisely.

"Afternoon, Kristol," greeted Michael, flashing a quick smile as he continued typing away on his laptop.

"Good afternoon," replied Kristol, her eyes scanning the room before she brought her focus back to the task at hand. "Today, we'll be reviewing the financial budgets for the upcoming fiscal year. As you know, this is a crucial part of our planning process, and I appreciate all the hard work you've put into these projections."

Kristol gestured to the screen, and Susan promptly connected her laptop to display the budget spreadsheets. The room bathed in the soft glow of the projected financial data.

Mark began the presentation by walking the team through revenue projections and discussing market trends that might impact their financial goals. Lisa followed, outlining the departmental budget allocations and highlighting areas where cost-cutting measures could be implemented without compromising performance.

Throughout the meeting, Kristol listened attentively, occasionally interjecting with questions and suggestions. Her leadership style was collaborative, and she encouraged her team to voice their ideas and concerns.

As they went deeper into the financial reports, Michael uncovered a potential opportunity for increasing revenue through a strategic partnership. Susan proposed a more efficient allocation of resources within their marketing department, which could lead to significant cost savings.

Kristol nodded in approval, appreciating the creativity and dedication of her team. She knew that their collective effort and insights were crucial for the company's financial success.

By the end of the meeting, they had reviewed every line item, made necessary adjustments, and had a more precise roadmap for the upcoming fiscal year. Kristol concluded the session with a sense of accomplishment and gratitude for her team's dedication.

"Thank you, everyone," she said with a smile. "This was a productive meeting. Let's reconvene in one month to review any adjustments and ensure our financial plans are on track. Until then, keep up the excellent work."

As the workday came to a close, Kristol gathered her belongings and made her way to her car in the dimly lit parking garage. The weight of the day's challenges was sitting on her shoulders, and she felt the familiar presence of fear eating away at the edges of her consciousness.

As she started her car and merged into the evening traffic, the world around her seemed to blur. The headlights of passing cars became streaks of light, and the honking horns and rush-hour chaos echoed in her ears like distant memories. Kristol's heart began to race, and her palms grew clammy as fear tightened its grip on her.

The side effects of the car accident were now an unwelcome reality. The world outside her car seemed to shift and warp, and Kristol struggled to maintain her focus on the road ahead. Fear whispered in her ear, taunting her with visions of accidents and disasters.

Kristol's hands clenched the steering wheel, her knuckles turning white as she tried to regain control of her racing thoughts. The happiness she had discovered in the flower shop and the wisdom she had gained from Citta felt like distant memories, overshadowed by the presence of fear.

In the midst of her panic, Kristol remembered the conversations she had received from Citta and Seth – to confront fear and embrace happiness. She took a deep breath, forcing herself to stay present and grounded. The traffic around her began to regain its normalcy, and the streaks of light transformed back into ordinary headlights.

As she continued her drive home, Kristol made a silent promise to herself – she would not let fear dictate her life.

After arriving home, Kristol was greeted by Max and Bella with warmth and affection. The enthusiastic wagging of their tails and barks filled the air as they rushed outside into the backyard for their evening playtime. Watching her dogs, Kristol couldn't help but feel a sense of emotional comfort, a brief reprieve from the challenges of the day.

Kristol retreated inside to her living room. She settled onto the couch and reached for her smartphone, turning it back on and checking her messages for missed calls and urgent notifications. Among the notifications was a call from her mother, and a sense of guilt washed over her for not having her phone on to return it earlier.

Kristol decided to dial her doctor's office number, but after several rings, she was met with a recorded voice, "Thank you for calling HealthLink Medical Center. Our office hours are from 9 AM to 5 PM, Monday through Friday. If you're calling outside of these hours or for non-urgent matters, please leave a message, and we'll get back to you as soon as possible. If this is an emergency, please hang up and dial 911."

Frustrated, Kristol hung up and decided to return her mother's call, hoping for some support and guidance. After a few rings, her mother's warm voice came through the line.

"Hello, sweetheart," her mother greeted her. "I was wondering when you'd have a moment to chat," annoyed that Kristol didn't call sooner.

"Hi, Mom," Kristol replied, her voice filled with genuine affection. "I'm sorry I missed your call earlier. It's been a busy day."

Her mother, not hiding her annoyance, said, "I understand. How are you holding up? Is everything okay?"

Kristol hesitated for a moment, contemplating whether to share her recent experiences and the challenges she was facing. She decided to be honest with her mother, someone she had always been able to confide in, regardless of her mother's sternness.

"I've been going through some changes, Mom," she began. "After the car accident, I've been experiencing...well, some side effects. It's been a bit overwhelming."

Her mother listened attentively, her caring presence evident even over the phone. "I'm sorry to hear that. Have you talked to your doctor about it?"

"I actually just tried calling my doctor's office," Kristol replied. "I want to schedule an appointment and see if there's a way to manage what I am experiencing."

They continued their conversation, discussing various aspects of Kristol's life, including her work and the upcoming Hawaiian barbecue at the office that weekend.

After saying goodbye to her mother and promising to keep her updated on her doctor's appointment, Kristol ended the call, dialed her doctor's office once more, and left a message. She knew that seeking professional guidance was essential.

Chapter Eight

THE COIN OF EMOTIONS

The next day, as Kristol was preparing for her office meeting, her phone rang. She glanced at the caller ID and saw it was HealthLink Medical, and she answered the call.

"Hello, this is Kristol," she said, her voice steady.

"Good morning, Kristol. This is Carmen from HealthLink Medical. I'm calling to schedule your appointment," the cheerful voice on the other end replied. "Who is your doctor?"

Kristol felt a sense of relief wash over her. "Good morning, Carmen. Thank you for getting back to me. My doctor is Dr. Baker."

"Dr. Baker has an opening tomorrow, Wednesday, at 10 AM due to a last-minute cancellation. Does that work for you?" Carmen asked.

Kristol checked her calendar quickly and confirmed, "Wednesday at 10 AM sounds perfect. Please go ahead and schedule it."

"Great! Your appointment with Dr. Baker is confirmed for Wednesday at 10 AM. Is there anything specific you'd like to discuss during the visit or any concerns you'd like us to note?"

Kristol hesitated for a moment, considering the recent fear and anxiety that had crept into her life. "Actually, Carmen, I've been feeling a bit overwhelmed lately. Could you make a note for Dr. Baker to address that during the appointment?"

"Of course, Kristol. We'll make sure to note that down. Is there anything else you'd like to add?" replied Carmen.

Kristol thought for a moment. "No, that should be it for now. Thank you."

"You're welcome, Kristol. We're here to help. If you have any questions or need further assistance before your appointment, don't hesitate to reach out. Have a great day!"

With the call ended, Kristol felt a sense of accomplishment. She had taken a step toward addressing her health concerns, and that gave her a glimmer of hope.

As the day unfolded, Kristol found herself engrossed in her work. The routine of corporate training sessions, presentations, and meetings provided a brief distraction from the fear that had taken residence in her mind.

However, as the hours passed, the anxiety began to resurface. Kristol couldn't help but feel the weight of uncertainty and the unknown pressing down on her. The fear seemed to grow stronger with each passing moment, threatening to overshadow any sense of happiness she had left.

By the time the workday was over, Kristol was mentally drained. She decided to go for a long walk with her dogs, hoping that the fresh air and the company of her furry friends would offer some solace.

As she strolled through the park, her mind kept returning to the upcoming doctor's appointment. The fear of what might be discovered cast darkness over her.

Kristol's dogs, sensing her unease, nuzzled closer to her. Their presence provided a small measure of relief, a reminder that there were simple joys in life that could still be found, even in the midst of fear.

Eventually, Kristol returned home. She decided to call Sarah. As she dialed the number and waited for Sarah to answer, she hoped for a reassuring voice on the other end of the line, someone who could provide a glimmer of light.

Kristol anxiously awaited as the phone rang. She needed a friend right now, someone who could understand the turmoil inside her. Finally, Sarah's familiar voice came through the receiver.

"Hey, Kristol, how's it going?" Sarah's voice was filled with energy as if she couldn't wait to share something.

Kristol hesitated for a moment, her anxiety still lingering. "Hey, Sarah," she began, her voice trembling slightly. "I... I need to talk to you about something. It's kind of important."

Sarah, caught up in her own world, didn't seem to notice the seriousness in Kristol's tone. "Of course, Kristol! But first, let me tell you about the latest update on the Hawaiian barbecue. It's going to be absolutely incredible! We've got so many fun activities planned, and the decorations are coming along beautifully."

Listening to Sarah's enthusiastic chatter about the upcoming barbecue, Kristol felt a pang of disappointment. She had hoped for a sympathetic ear, someone who would listen to her fears and concerns. Instead, it seemed that Sarah was preoccupied with her own excitement.

"Sarah, I'm glad you're excited about the barbecue," Kristol interrupted gently. "But there's something I really need to talk to you about. It's... well, it's about my health."

Sarah paused for a moment, her tone shifting slightly. "Oh, health stuff, Kristol? Can't it wait a bit? I promise I'll listen, but I have a lot on my plate right now with the barbecue preparations. You understand, right?"

Kristol felt frustration and disappointment. She had hoped for a friend who would prioritize her well-being over party planning. "I understand, Sarah, but this is really important to me. I'm just feeling a bit scared and overwhelmed, and I could use some support."

Sarah's response was not what Kristol had hoped for. "I get it, Kristol, but I promise we'll talk about it soon, okay? Right now, I've got to finalize the luau playlist and coordinate with the caterer. You know how it is when you're in charge of these events."

Kristol sighed softly, realizing that Sarah's focus was elsewhere. "Okay, Sarah, I understand. Just let me know when you're ready to talk. Thanks."

Kristol couldn't help but feel a sense of loneliness and frustration. She had reached out for support, and while Sarah hadn't been entirely dismissive, she also hadn't fully acknowledged the depth of Kristol's concerns.

Kristol arrived at HealthLink Medical on Wednesday morning as the bright sun shone through the dense smog. She had spent the previous night tossing and turning, her mind filled with worries about the upcoming doctor's appointment. As she stepped into the clinic, she couldn't shake the feeling of unease that had settled in the pit of her stomach.

The reception area was calm, with soft music playing in the background and a friendly receptionist at the front desk. Kristol approached the desk, her hands trembling slightly.

"Good morning," the receptionist greeted her with a warm smile. "How can I assist you today?"

Kristol cleared her throat, trying to steady her nerves. "I have an appointment with Dr. Baker at 10 am. My name is Kristol Davis."

The receptionist checked her computer and nodded. "Ah, yes, Ms. Davis. Dr. Baker will be with you shortly. Please have a seat in the waiting area, and we'll call you in when he's ready."

Kristol took a deep breath and found an empty chair in the waiting area. She glanced around, her eyes lingering on the other patients, each lost in their own thoughts and concerns. The minutes ticked by slowly, and the anxiety that had plagued her intensified.

Finally, the door to Dr. Baker's office opened, and a nurse called out, "Kristol Davis?"

Kristol stood up, her heart pounding, and followed the nurse into the examination room.

Kristol sat in the examination room, the ticking of the clock on the wall amplifying her anxiety. She fidgeted with a pamphlet on the table, her thoughts racing. Finally, the door opened, and Dr. Baker walked in, greeting her with a warm smile.

"Hi, Kristol. It's good to see you again." Dr. Baker said, extending his hand. "How are you today?"

Kristol shook his hand and managed a weak smile. "I've been better, doctor. I've been dealing with some health issues lately, and it's been causing me a lot of stress."

Dr. Baker nodded understandingly. "I see. Well, we're here to help you find answers and solutions. Please, have a seat, and we'll discuss your concerns."

Kristol sat down, her anxiety still palpable. She proceeded to share her symptoms, her fears, and the overwhelming sense of dread that had been plaguing her in recent weeks. Dr. Baker listened attentively, jotting down notes as she spoke.

After a thorough examination and a series of questions, Dr. Baker finally spoke, his tone gentle but direct. "Kristol, based on your symptoms and what you've described, it seems like you're dealing with a combination of anxiety and depression. These conditions can have implications, affecting both your mental and physical well-being."

Kristol's eyes welled up with tears as the weight of the diagnosis settled in. She had suspected as much, but hearing it from a medical professional made it all too real.

Dr. Baker continued, "I want you to know that you're not alone in this, Kristol. Many people face similar challenges, especially after traumatic events, and there are treatments available that can help you manage your symptoms and improve your quality of life."

He explained that he would prescribe an anti-depressant to help alleviate her anxiety and depression, and he also recommended counseling or therapy to address the underlying emotional issues.

Kristol nodded, her voice shaky. "I appreciate your guidance. It's just... it's been so overwhelming, and I didn't know where to turn."

Kristol stepped out of the doctor's office, a prescription in her hand. The appointment had been reassuring, and Dr. Baker's prescription for anti-depressants left her feeling a glimmer of hope. She made her way to her car, her mind still processing the visit.

As she settled into the driver's seat, a new and unfamiliar emotion washed over her. It was as if a subtle breeze of determination had blown through her thoughts, dispelling some of the darkness that had clouded her mind. Instead of heading directly to the pharmacy to fill her prescription, she found herself turning the steering wheel in a different direction.

The flower district.

The decision surprised her even as she made it. She couldn't explain why she felt compelled to go there, but it was as if an invisible force was guiding her steps.

As Kristol navigated the familiar streets of the city, she couldn't help but reflect on her recent journey. The car accident, the dream-like world, the encounter with Citta, and now the doctor's appointment—it all seemed like pieces of a puzzle slowly coming together. She couldn't deny that something had shifted within her, a subtle transformation that defied rational explanation.

Arriving at the flower district, Kristol parked her car and stepped out onto the active streets. The lively colors and intoxicating scents of the flowers surrounded her, bringing back memories. She began to stroll along the rows of stalls, admiring the exotic flowers from different corners of the world.

As she walked, she couldn't shake the feeling that she was on the verge of a discovery. It was as if the flowers held the key to something important, something that had eluded her for so long. She reached out to touch a velvety petal, feeling its softness beneath her fingertips.

A voice from behind startled her. "Beautiful, aren't they?"

Kristol turned to see a middle-aged woman with a warm smile. She was dressed in vibrant, flowing clothes that seemed to blend seamlessly with the colorful surroundings.

"Yes, they are," Kristol replied.

The woman approached; her eyes filled with a knowing light. "You're not just here for the flowers, are you?"

Kristol hesitated for a moment, then found herself nodding. "No, I'm not. I... I don't know why I'm here, exactly. It's like something drew me back to this place."

The woman's smile deepened. "Ah, my dear, you've been called."

"Called?" Kristol questioned.

"Yes," the woman said, her tone filled with gentle assurance. "You see, the flowers are more than just beautiful decorations. They are messengers, conduits of energy, and wisdom keepers. And you, my dear, have a connection to this world, a connection that goes beyond reality."

Kristol's heart raced as she tried to comprehend the woman's words. "A connection? What do you mean?"

The woman's eyes held a depth of knowing as she gently guided Kristol toward a particular flower stand. Kristol followed her lead, her heart pounding, mixed with emotions.

As they approached the familiar stand, Kristol noticed a figure standing amidst the vibrant blossoms. It was Isa, the woman who had initially invited her to cross through the arching trees. Their eyes met, and an unspoken understanding passed between them. Kristol knew that this meeting was no coincidence.

In silence, Kristol and Isa exchanged a nod, acknowledging the bond that had formed between them. There was no need for words; their connection transcended language. With a sense of purpose, Kristol walked under the arching trees, feeling the world around her shift and shimmer once more.

On the other side of the threshold, she found herself in a place that was both familiar and utterly transformed once again. The colors were radiant, the scents pulsating with aroma, full of life. It was a place where everything coexisted in perfect harmony.

From behind her, Citta's warm voice broke the silence. "You see, Kristol," she began, "in this world, intentions and emotions have the power to shape reality. Remember, what you feel and believe becomes your truth. It's a place where the energy of creation flows freely, and you have the opportunity to tap into it."

Kristol turned to find Citta standing there; her presence was an aura of serenity and joy. She greeted Citta with a smile, feeling a deep sense of gratitude for the guidance she had received thus far.

Citta continued, her words carrying the weight of insight. "But there's something more, Kristol. We understand the perception of emotions. You see, if fear exists, so does happiness. It's like a coin with two sides, like a quarter. On one side, you have fear, with all its shadows and uncertainties. But flip that coin, and there's happiness, gleaming with its radiant light. Our subconscious tends to focus on one side, but the other is always present, waiting to be acknowledged."

Kristol's forehead creased, intrigued by Citta's words. "So, you mean that even in the presence of fear, there is the potential for happiness?"

Citta nodded, her expression playful. "Exactly! Imagine it like this: Life is like a comedy show, and our emotions are the actors on stage. Fear plays its part, and so does happiness. They are polar opposites, performing their roles in this grand production we call life."

Kristol couldn't help but smile at Citta's whimsical analogy. "So, you're saying that we have the power to choose which emotion takes center stage in our lives?"

Citta's laughter echoed like music. "Precisely! Imagine this as a stand-up comedy routine. Sometimes, fear gets a bit too carried away with its performance, and it's up to us to bring in the comedic happiness to lighten the mood. It's about finding the humor in our quirks and imperfections."

Kristol found herself captivated by Citta's words. "But how do we do that? How do we shift our focus from fear to happiness?"

Citta paused, her gaze fixed on a cluster of radiant flowers nearby. "Ah, my dear, that's where the magic of this world comes into play. It's about embracing the beauty and wonder that surrounds us, like these exquisite flowers." She gestured to the sparkling blossoms. "Every petal, every color, every fragrance carries a story of creation and joy. When we immerse ourselves in this world, we open the door to a different perspective, a perspective where happiness can take the spotlight."

Kristol took in the intoxicating smells of the flowers that surrounded them, feeling a sense of peace. It was as if the very essence of happiness was woven into this realm.

Citta continued, her voice filled with gentle wisdom. "Remember, Kristol, life may throw us challenges and moments of fear, but it also offers us the gift of laughter and happiness. It's all a matter of where we choose to direct our focus."

Kristol nodded, absorbing Citta's teachings. "I want to learn how to shift my focus, to embrace happiness even in the face of fear. But how do I begin?"

Citta placed a reassuring hand on Kristol's shoulder. "It starts with awareness, my dear. Acknowledge when fear takes the stage, but don't let it take over the comedy of life. Find the moments of laughter and joy, then let them shine. And always remember, if there's going to be a life review, it might as well be a comedy rather than a drama."

As they walked, Citta began to share an analogy, this time with a circus twist.

"Life is a bit like a circus," Citta began mischievously. "Sometimes, we find ourselves walking on a tightrope, balancing fear and uncertainty with every step we take. It's as if we're teetering on the edge, wondering if we'll make it to the other side without falling."

Kristol nodded in agreement, her mind visualizing the precarious act of a tightrope walker. "Yes, I've felt that way many times, especially in my career."

Citta continued, "But here's the beauty of it: just when fear threatens to steal the show, the circus clowns come rushing in. They stumble, they fall, and they make us laugh with their silly slapstick humor. I mean, who rides miniature bicycles while juggling balls in funny costumes while trying to fit 15 clowns in a tiny car, all at the same time?"

Kristol couldn't help but laugh at Citta's words. "You're right, Citta. It's like we have these inner clowns that can turn our fear-filled circus into a funny comedy."

There was a profound simplicity in her teachings; life is meant to be lived with a sense of lightness and humor.

Citta grinned. "Exactly! Life's circus is a blend of suspense and laughter, and it's up to us to decide who takes the spotlight. Sometimes, we need those inner clowns to remind us that it's okay to stumble and laugh at ourselves. In the midst of our fears," Citta continued, "there's room for joy and happiness. It's only a matter of perspective where we focus."

Turning to Citta, Kristol was about to ask her next question. Before she could utter a word, Citta simply vanished as easily as she had appeared. Kristol blinked in surprise; her surroundings momentarily blurred by the sudden departure. She looked around, searching for any trace of Citta, but there was no sign of her.

It was as if Citta had melted into the very essence, leaving behind the laughter-filled echoes of her teachings. Kristol couldn't help but feel a touch of sadness at the unexpected parting. She had so many questions, so much more to learn, but it seemed that for now, the guidance of Citta had come to an end.

As Kristol drove away, the flower district slowly faded in her rearview mirror. With each passing mile, the demands and responsibilities of her corporate job started to weigh on her once more. The fear that had briefly receded now returned, its grip tightening on her heart. Thoughts of budgets, deadlines, and the relentless pursuit of success hovered ominously.

And then there was the doctor's prescription, a possible solution to the inner battles she had been facing. It had slipped her mind amidst the enchantment of the flower district and the teachings of Citta. The medication was meant to help her combat the relentless fear that threatened to consume her.

After work, Kristol strolled through the park with her dogs, always eager for their daily outing, trotting ahead, tails wagging happily. As she wandered through the park, the colors looked different. Flowers of every hue burst forth from the meticulously tended garden beds, their fragrant aromas filling the air. It was a sight she had never paid much attention to before, but this evening, it drew her in like a magnet.

Approaching the garden, Kristol felt a sense of déjà vu. Kneeling beside a bed of roses, Kristol inhaled deeply. It was as if the world around her faded into the background. For a moment, she was transported back to where happiness and laughter were as genuine as the flowers themselves.

Just as she was lost in her reverie, a burst of playful energy from her dogs broke the spell. Her furry companions had discovered a squirrel darting through the trees. Kristol laughed at their antics; their unbridled joy lightened her heart. It was then that she noticed Liam approaching, his own dog in tow.

"Looks like they're having quite the adventure," Liam remarked, his voice friendly and inviting.

Kristol nodded, still amused by her dogs' antics. "Yes, they certainly know how to make the most of a day at the park."

Liam's dog, a lively retriever, bounded over to join Kristol's pups in their game of chase, and the three dogs frolicked together.

They watched their dogs with shared amusement for a moment before Liam spoke again. "You know, there's something about this place, isn't there? The flowers, the energy... it's like a little slice of paradise in the middle of the city."

Kristol's eyes sparkled with recognition. "You feel it, too?"

Liam nodded, a serene smile gracing his lips. "Absolutely. Every time I come here, it's like a breath of fresh air for the soul. Beauty is all around us if we take the time to notice."

As they both soaked in the tranquil atmosphere of the flower garden, Kristol couldn't help but agree. "You're right, Liam. It's moments like these that make life truly special.

"Any fun weekend plans?" Asked Liam.

Kristol, grateful for the change of topic, shared. "Well, Sarah, my best friend, is running around like a hurricane, trying to make the annual office barbecue the event of the summer. She's got all these grand plans for the luau theme, and I'm not sure if the office is ready for my hula dancing skills."

Liam laughed heartily. "Hula dancing, huh? That's something I'd love to see. Don't forget to invite me to the next dance practice!"

Their banter continued, easing any tensions from the day. Kristol was grateful for Liam's presence in her life and the joy to be found in simple conversations and shared laughter.

Chapter Nine

A SWANKY EVENING

♥

Sarah's voice sounded cheerful and inviting over the phone. "Hey, Kristol! I was thinking, why wait for the office luau to have some fun? There's a wine and art gallery event downtown this Friday night. How about we kick off the weekend with a little culture and relaxation?"

Kristol considered the idea for a moment, her mind torn between work-related concerns and the need for a break. "That sounds like a great idea, Sarah. But you know the office luau is the next day, and I've been a bit tired."

Sarah chuckled. "I get it, but sometimes, a little break before a big event can do wonders. Plus, it's not like we'll be partying all night. Just a few hours of art, wine, and good company. What do you say?"

Kristol hesitated, the weight of her responsibilities pressing down on her. She glanced at her calendar, filled with reminders and tasks. Then, she thought about the flower district and the encounter with Citta, the laughter and wisdom shared. Maybe a short break would be exactly what she needed to shift her perspective.

Finally, she smiled. "You know what, Sarah? You're right. Let's do it. A night of art and wine sounds like the perfect prelude to our weekend luau."

Sarah enthusiastically said, "That's the spirit, Kristol! It'll be a great way to unwind and get into the luau spirit. I'll pick you up around 7 pm on Friday. Dress comfortably but with a touch of artsy flair. We'll be meeting some friends there. It's going to be fantastic!"

As the Friday night sun began to set, Sarah arrived at Kristol's doorstep promptly at 7:00. The two friends exchanged smiles and greetings and set off for a night of fun. The anticipation of an evening filled with art, wine, and the company of friends brought a sense of excitement.

When they arrived, they found themselves in a swanky winery with an adjoining art gallery. The ambiance was warm and inviting, with soft lighting casting a gentle glow over the artwork displayed on the walls. It was an oasis of creativity and relaxation.

Sarah led Kristol to a group of women who were already gathered in a corner of the gallery. The women were acquaintances from various walks of life, each with their own unique stories and experiences.

Amanda, the vibrant artist, greeted Kristol with a warm smile. "Welcome! It's so lovely to meet you. I'm Amanda," she said.

Lydia, the well-traveled journalist, extended her hand. "Hi there, I'm Lydia," she introduced herself. "I can't wait to hear your stories and share some of mine. There's always an adventure waiting to be told, isn't there?"

Elena, the eco-conscious entrepreneur, joined in. "Hello, I'm Elena," she said with a friendly nod. "I'm all about sustainable fashion and making a positive impact on the planet. It's great to have you here."

Sarah turned to Kristol and introduced her to the group with a warm smile. "Everyone, I'd like you to meet my dear friend, Kristol," she said. "Kristol is a corporate trainer and one of the most genuine people you'll ever meet."

As the evening continued, the group of women found themselves engaged in lively conversation. The soft strains of music wafted through the air, creating a soothing backdrop for their exchange.

Amanda began the conversation with a question. "So, Kristol, tell us more about your work as a corporate trainer. It sounds fascinating."

Kristol smiled and leaned in, feeling a sense of connection already. "I help organizations develop their employees' skills and capabilities. It's all about empowering individuals to reach their full potential within the company. I find it incredibly rewarding."

Lydia nodded in understanding. "Empowerment is such an important aspect of personal and professional growth, especially for women. I can see why you enjoy your work."

Elena, the eco-conscious entrepreneur, chimed in, her eyes bright with curiosity. "And how do you incorporate sustainability and ethical practices into your training programs?"

Kristol's face lit up as she shared her passion for conscious business practices. "I firmly believe that businesses should not only be successful but also socially responsible. I encourage companies to adopt sustainable strategies, from leadership development to employee engagement."

Sarah, who had known Kristol for years, added her perspective. "Kristol's commitment to making a positive impact in the corporate world is truly inspiring." Sarah, sensing the need for a change in the conversation's direction, raised her wineglass, "Ladies, let's declare tonight a night of pure fun and enjoyment, a night where we set aside our work-related discussions and simply have fun. What do you say?"

The group responded with cheers and laughter, agreeing wholeheartedly to the idea of a work-free evening. With that decision made, the conversation shifted to lighter topics, allowing everyone to connect on a more personal level.

Amanda leaned forward with enthusiasm. "Alright, then! Let's kick things off with a question. What's everyone's favorite book of all time? I'll start—I'm a sucker for anything that is romance related."

As the women continued their lively conversation, Amanda's admiration for romance prompted Lydia to share her literary preference.

Lydia leaned forward with a thoughtful expression. "You know, Amanda, while I appreciate romance, my heart leans more towards personal development. The ability to blend spirituality, philosophy, and storytelling is simply enchanting."

Amanda nodded in understanding. "Ah, yes, personal development resonates with so many readers. It's amazing how literature can touch our souls in different ways."

Elena shared her preference. "I'm all about personal growth for me as well, especially in the business-conscious world.

Their animated conversation paused momentarily as the waiter returned with a fresh glass of wine, a polite smile gracing his face. "Here you go, ladies," he said cheerfully. Please enjoy your evening."

As he departed with a graceful nod, the women resumed their chat, raising their glasses in a silent toast to the pleasures of the night.

Amanda asked, "Kristol, what have you been reading lately?"

Kristol felt a moment of hesitation as the question reached her ears. She knew that her recent experiences had shifted her priorities and interests, and it was time to be honest about it.

She looked at Amanda and admitted, "Honestly, Amanda, I haven't been reading much lately, especially since my car accident. I've been spending a lot of time in the park with my dogs, just enjoying the simplicity of it all." Kristol admitted. "There's something incredibly soothing about the sound of leaves rustling in the wind and the scent of flowers in bloom."

Elena nodded appreciatively. "Doesn't Nature have a way of healing the soul? It's a beautiful way to find peace."

As Kristol engaged in the lively conversation, guilt nagged at her. She realized that she had been revisiting the flower district and experiencing these intriguing encounters without sharing a word of it with Sarah. The flower district had become a secret world, one that Kristol chose to keep to herself.

She pondered the reasons for her silence. Perhaps it was the fear of not being understood, of sounding too strange or "woo-woo." Or maybe it was because she was still trying to make sense of it all, unsure of how to put these extraordinary experiences into words. Regardless of the reasons, she knew that she couldn't keep this hidden world to herself forever. The time would come when she would have to share it with Sarah, no matter how unbelievable it might sound.

For now, though, Kristol decided to revel in the camaraderie of her new friends, savoring the moments of laughter and connection they were all sharing. It was a night of fun, as Sarah had suggested, and she was determined to make the most of it.

As the evening wore on, the music in the winery shifted to a livelier tune. Amanda couldn't resist the rhythm and stood up, extending a hand to Kristol. "Come on, Kristol! Let's dance."

Kristol, usually reserved in social settings, couldn't resist Amanda's invitation, and the two of them joined the impromptu dance floor. The other women soon followed suit, and the group twirled and swayed to the music, letting loose and enjoying the moment.

As they danced and laughed together, Kristol felt a sense of belonging she hadn't experienced in a long time. The evening had started with an invitation to a wine and art event, then transformed into a beautiful connection with a group of incredible women who shared her passion for life.

Back at their table, the group of women found themselves engrossed in lively conversation that meandered through topics ranging from art and literature to travel and hobbies. The atmosphere was filled with light-hearted fun, and it was evident that these women were quickly forming a bond.

Amidst the exchange of stories and experiences, a woman approached their table bearing a stack of colorful flyers. She carefully distributed one to each of the women, who looked at the unexpected additions to their evening.

Lydia, always quick to investigate, was the first to speak up. "What's this?" she mused aloud, holding up the flyer for the others to see. The flyer depicted a tranquil desert scene with a resort and reflection pool in the center. In an elegant script, it read: "Embrace your Inner Self: The Path to Transformation."

Amanda, intrigued by the imagery, studied the flyer closely. "It looks like some sort of retreat," she observed. "A getaway, perhaps?"

Elena, who was always conscious of sustainable and eco-friendly experiences, scrutinized the flyer for details. "It's essential that it promotes environmental responsibility."

Sarah took a flyer and examined it with interest. "This could be a great opportunity for all of us to recharge and relax," she suggested. "We've all been so busy with our respective lives. A retreat might be just what we need."

Kristol read the flyer with growing interest. She couldn't help but wonder if this retreat might hold the key to unlocking more of the mysteries and wisdom she had encountered in the flower district. The thought of a week's retreat resonated with her deeply.

Before anyone could voice their thoughts further, the woman returned, offering a brief explanation. "Ladies, this flyer is for a week retreat organized by the gallery," she explained. "It's an opportunity for participants to connect with themselves and their emotions, explore their creativity, and embark on a creative journey of self-discovery. The gallery has partnered with experienced facilitators to ensure a meaningful and rejuvenating experience."

The flyers were set aside while Kristol carefully tucked hers into her purse to look at a bit later.

Sarah suddenly glanced at her watch and exclaimed, "Oh my goodness, Kristol, we need to get going! Tomorrow is going to be a full day with the office barbecue. We should get some rest."

Kristol nodded in agreement, realizing that the weekend was about to kick off with a bright and early morning. She rose from her seat, her purse slung over her shoulder, and bid a warm farewell to the group of women she had just met.

"Thank you all for a wonderful evening," she said with a smile. "I look forward to our next gathering and maybe even that retreat."

The women echoed their sentiments of excitement and anticipation, and as Kristol and Sarah made their way toward the exit, Amanda called out, "Take care, you two! Enjoy the barbecue."

Kristol and Sarah stepped out into the night. The air was cool and refreshing, a reminder that the city held many more surprises and possibilities than they could have imagined.

As they walked to their car, the sounds of the city at night surrounded them—soft laughter, distant music, and the gentle hum of life. Kristol couldn't help but reflect on the unexpected turns her life had taken recently. Little did she know that the weekend would bring even more twists and revelations, leading her further along the path of self-discovery and transformation.

Chapter Ten

THE POWER OF DUALITY

♥

As Kristol awoke on Saturday morning, she found herself tangled in a web of fitful dreams. Fear had been lurking within her, manifesting in the restless sleep. The energy clung to her like a thick, gooey, black tar substance, weighing her down and suffocating her.

She lay in bed for a moment as the remnants of the nightmares haunted her thoughts. It felt as though a dark, oozing lava sludge was blackening the normally bright sunny day.

With a deep breath, Kristol tried to shake off the feelings and recalled she forgot to fill her prescription for the antidepressants that the doctor gave her. She knew that dwelling on those unsettling dreams would only serve to fuel her anxiety. Instead, she attempted to focus on the present moment, the soft morning light filtering through her curtains and the sound of birds chirping outside.

Slowly, she eased herself out of bed and began her morning routine. Fear persisted like a ghost haunting a house.

Kristol reminded herself of the techniques she had learned over the years to manage her anxiety. Deep breaths, positive affirmations, and visualization exercises were all tools she had used in the past. She would need them now more than ever.

Descending the stairs to the kitchen, Kristol prepared a cup of coffee and sat down at the table. She closed her eyes for a moment, focusing on her breath, and repeated affirmations in an attempt to calm her racing thoughts. However, nothing seemed to work. Fear remained a stubborn presence, refusing to let go.

As Kristol sat there with frustration mounting, she suddenly recalled what Citta had said at the flower shop – something about there being two sides to a quarter, one opposite to the other. Her memory sparked, and she jumped up from the table, determined to find a quarter to examine.

Rummaging through a nearby drawer, Kristol finally located a shiny quarter. She held it in her hand, her fingers tracing the familiar ridges along the edges. As she studied the coin, she remembered Citta's words with clarity.

"It's like a coin with two sides," Citta had said. "Our subconscious tends to focus on one side, but the other is always present, waiting to be acknowledged."

Kristol stared at the quarter, contemplating the wisdom hidden within this simple object. The realization hit her like a bolt of lightning – her mind had been focusing solely on one side of the coin, the side consumed by fear and anxiety. But what about the other side? What was she neglecting to acknowledge?

With determination, Kristol decided to explore this idea further. She knew that fear was a part of her, but it wasn't the only part. There were other emotions, other aspects of herself that she needed to recognize and embrace. It was time to flip the coin and discover what lay on the opposite side.

Taking a deep breath, Kristol closed her eyes once more and began to move inward with her thoughts and feelings. She allowed herself to acknowledge the flip side, such as courage, resilience, and the strength that also resided within her. It was challenging, but she was determined to confront the other side of the coin and find happiness.

As she sat there, the scent of coffee filling the room, Kristol felt a subtle shift within her. The fear had not vanished, but it no longer dominated her every thought and emotion. She had taken the first step in acknowledging the duality, fear, and happiness.

The phone rang, jolting Kristol from her reflective moment with the quarter. She blinked, momentarily disoriented, before reaching for the phone. The caller ID displayed her sister Emily's name. With a faint smile, Kristol answered the call.

"Hey, Em," she greeted, her voice with surprise and warmth.

"Kristol! Long time no talk!" Emily's voice came through the line, uplifting and energetic as ever. "I was just thinking about our last tennis match. Mom said you are getting the brace off soon. Ready for a rematch?"

Kristol chuckled, her sister's competitive streak always managing to bring a smile to her face. "You never give up, do you?"

Emily snickered. "That's what makes it fun! So, what do you say?"

Kristol stared at the quarter still resting on the table. She realized that her sister's competitive nature had always been a part of their relationship, just as fear was a part of her own existence. But there was more to their connection than just competition.

"Sure, Em," Kristol replied, her voice filled with a sense of acceptance and affection. "I'm up for a rematch anytime, but I still need to take it easy. But let's make it more than just a game this time."

Emily asked, "What do you have in mind?"

"Remember, Em," Kristol said, her voice filled with nostalgia, "how we used to pretend there were secret messages in the tennis balls and the net was the gateway to another world? Let's play that magical game again; it's time to relive those moments of joy and connection, just like we used to. We had so much fun doing that."

Emily chuckled, the fond memories echoing in her own heart. "Yes, and we'd make up stories about the imaginary kingdom on the other side of the net. Every point was a new chapter in our epic tale."

Kristol smiled, her sister's words resonating deeply. "It wasn't just about winning or losing. It was about the playfulness, the creativity, and the sister bond we shared. We should bring some of that magic back into our match."

Emily agreed wholeheartedly. "Absolutely! Let's make it an adventure, just like old times. —keeping score, of course!"

As Kristol and Emily continued to discuss their upcoming tennis match, Emily's voice filled with enthusiasm, and she said, "How about we schedule the match for 2:00 PM today? I promise I will keep it easy on you. It's a perfect time to relive those memories."

Kristol paused for a moment, her brow scrunching, "I wish I could, Em, but I can't do 2:00 PM today. I have the Hawaiian office party later this afternoon – and don't forget, I need my brace to come off first, doctor's orders."

Before Emily could respond, chaos erupted in the background. Kristol's two dogs, Max and Bella, woke up and burst into a frenzy of excitement. They started racing around the house, playing a game of chase that seemed to involve every corner of the living room.

The dogs' playfulness filled the air, making it difficult for Kristol to hear Emily on the other end of the line. The doggy door became a focal point of their game, with Max and Bella taking turns darting in and out, causing loud banging.

Emily burst into laughter on the other end of the line, the sound echoing with amusement. "Sounds like you have your hands full with those two troublemakers! No worries, Kristol. We can reschedule for another day. Just let me know when you're free – but let's play soon," Emily pressured.

Kristol finally managed to calm Max and Bella down, but not without a bit of a struggle. "Thanks, Em. I'll find a time that works for both of us. And you're right, these two are a handful, but I wouldn't have it any other way."

As the day wore on, Kristol found herself caught up in the preparations for the Hawaiian office party. The thought of a fun-filled evening with colleagues and clients was exciting, but the fear from her restless night still weighed on her mind. Reflecting on her conversation with Emily, Kristol couldn't help but appreciate the dynamic of duality in life – the balance between competition and friendship, between fear and courage, and between the past and the present.

Kristol went to get ready for the day and chose a beautiful floral-printed dress. She carefully braided her hair, leaving a few loose strands to frame her face. She wanted to look her best for the event, but as she applied makeup, her thoughts kept drifting back to the conversations with Citta and the inner wisdom lessons about fear and happiness.

Just as Kristol was finishing up her preparations, her phone rang, and she saw Sarah's name. She answered with a cheerful tone, "Hey, Sarah, what's up?"

Sarah's voice came through with a sense of urgency. "Kristol, I need your help. The setup for the party is taking longer than expected, and we could use an extra pair of hands. Can you come a bit earlier than planned?"

Kristol glanced at the clock. She had some time to spare before the party officially started. "Of course, Sarah. I'll be there as soon as I can. Is there anything specific you need me to do?"

Sarah explained the situation, detailing various tasks that needed assistance. From setting up tiki torches to arranging tables and decorations, there was plenty to be done to transform the park into a Hawaiian paradise.

Kristol agreed to help and quickly finished her preparations. She grabbed her car keys and made her way to the park, where the party preparations were in full swing. The park was located conveniently near the financial district, making it an ideal location for an after-work event.

Upon arrival, Kristol was greeted by the sight of colleagues and coworkers moving about, all dressed in colorful Hawaiian attire. The atmosphere was filled with excitement and anticipation. She spotted Sarah coordinating the setup with a clipboard in hand.

"Kristol, you're a lifesaver," Sarah said with a grateful smile. "We've got a lot to do, but with your help, I'm confident we'll get everything ready in time."

Kristol jumped into action, joining the team in transforming the park into a tropical paradise. As they worked together, her worries began to fade. The decorations, the scent of Hawaiian cuisine wafting through the air, and the laughter of her colleagues all contributed to the festive atmosphere.

With the preparations complete, Kristol and Sarah shared a moment of satisfaction. "We did it," Sarah exclaimed. "Thanks to your help, everything looks amazing. Now, let's enjoy the party!"

Kristol nodded, her heart lighter than it had been earlier in the day. She realized that despite the fears that had plagued her, the black tar was lifting off. Kristol was surrounded by friends and colleagues and the promise of a joyful evening ahead.

As the office party kicked off, Kristol found herself in the midst of a lively crowd. Colleagues and clients mingled, laughter and conversation filled the air, and the scent of delicious Hawaiian cuisine tantalized the senses.

Kristol was engrossed in a conversation with Seth and a group of associates, discussing a recent project they had been working on. The moment everyone had been waiting for arrived when the Executive team stepped onto the stage. The crowd hushed in anticipation as Matt Anderson took the microphone. He exuded charisma and authority, his words carrying weight and importance.

"Ladies and gentlemen, colleagues, clients," Matt Anderson began, his voice projecting out toward everyone. "I want to extend a warm welcome to all of you for joining us today at this fantastic Hawaiian barbecue. It's an opportunity for us to come together, celebrate our achievements, and show our appreciation."

The crowd responded with enthusiastic applause, and Matt continued, "I'd like to take a moment to express our heartfelt gratitude to someone special among us. This event, this amazing surprise coming up, was orchestrated by one of our own, Sarah Williams." He gestured to Sarah, who was sitting with Kristol and the others. Sarah blushed but beamed with pride as her coworkers clapped and cheered for her.

"Sarah has put her heart and soul into making this day memorable for all of us," he continued. "Her dedication and tireless efforts have not gone unnoticed, and we are grateful for her contributions."

The crowd erupted in applause once again, and Sarah's smile widened. Kristol couldn't help but feel a surge of pride for her friend. Sarah had indeed outdone herself in organizing this spectacular event.

Just as the applause began to die down, the lights dimmed, and the rhythmic beat of drums echoed through the park. The employees turned their attention back to the stage as a Hawaiian band, complete with ukuleles, steel guitars, and traditional drums, emerged. The musicians started to play enchanting music that transported everyone to a tropical paradise.

Then, the real surprise came as fire dancers appeared, their flaming torches twirling and casting mesmerizing patterns of light and shadow. The crowd watched in awe as the dancers moved gracefully, their fiery performance a dazzling spectacle against the night sky.

Kristol glanced around the park while the music was playing; she spotted a familiar figure in the distance. It was Citta, the mysterious woman who had appeared to her in the flower shop. Her heart fluttered as she excused herself from Seth and the others.

Kristol couldn't resist the urge to approach Citta to seek answers to the questions that had been plaguing her since their encounter. With determination in her stride, she began to weave her way through the lively crowd, making her way toward the woman who had left a lasting impression on her.

But as she drew closer, something strange happened. Citta seemed to shimmer and waver like a mirage in the distance. Kristol quickened her pace, her curiosity and longing moving her forward, but the closer she got, the more Citta's form seemed to blur and dissipate.

In a matter of seconds, Kristol reached the spot where she had seen Citta, only to find that there was no one there. It was as if the woman had vanished into thin air, leaving Kristol standing in the space, feeling disappointment and confusion.

Just as Kristol was about to turn and rejoin her associates, she accidentally bumped into someone who had been standing nearby. Startled, she looked up to see a man with a friendly smile. He extended a hand to steady her.

"I'm so sorry," Kristol apologized, feeling a bit flustered. "I didn't see where I was going."

The man, whose name tag identified him as Benjamin, chuckled good-naturedly. "No problem at all. It happens in crowded places like this. Are you enjoying the party?"

Kristol nodded, still somewhat distracted by her unsuccessful attempt to reach Citta. "Yes, it's a fantastic event. I just... thought I saw someone I needed to speak to."

Benjamin raised an eyebrow. "Someone important, I take it?"

Kristol hesitated for a moment, unsure of how much to reveal. "Yes, someone who influenced me. But it seems like they've disappeared."

Benjamin's expression turned thoughtful. "Sometimes, people come into our lives for a brief moment, leaving us with valuable lessons or insights. Perhaps this person served their purpose by showing you something important."

Kristol couldn't help but wonder if Benjamin was right. Maybe Citta's appearance had been a fleeting but powerful reminder of the lessons about fear and happiness. She decided to let go of her disappointment and focus on enjoying the party and the connections she was making.

Kristol considered Benjamin's words and found herself nodding in agreement. "You're absolutely right."

Benjamin smiled warmly. Realizing they hadn't properly introduced themselves, Kristol extended her hand. "I'm Kristol Davis, by the way. It's nice to meet you."

Benjamin shook her hand with a friendly grip. "Pleasure to meet you, Kristol. I'm Benjamin Miller. Are you a colleague of the firm or one of the clients?"

Kristol explained, "I am one of the corporate trainers for the firm. And you?"

Benjamin grinned. "I'm a client, one of the fortunate ones invited to this fantastic event. This party is quite the bonus."

Kristol smiled appreciatively at Benjamin. "Thank you for the pleasant conversation, Benjamin. It was a pleasure meeting you."

Benjamin returned her smile. "Likewise, Kristol. Enjoy the rest of the party, and maybe we'll cross paths again."

With a nod, Kristol gracefully excused herself from the conversation and made her way back to her group of friends. She rejoined Sarah, Seth, and the others.

Sarah decided it was the perfect moment to make an announcement. She excused herself from the table where she had been enjoying her meal with Kristol and other coworkers and headed towards the stage.

Kristol watched as Sarah approached the stage with a confident stride. She couldn't help but admire her friend's ability to take charge of a situation and captivate an audience. Once Sarah reached the stage, she tapped the microphone to capture everyone's attention. The crowd gradually fell silent, eager to hear what Sarah had to say.

"Good evening, everyone!" Sarah began, her voice projecting with enthusiasm. "I hope you're all having an amazing time at our Hawaiian luau. I have some exciting news to share that will make this event even more memorable." The employees turned their full attention to Sarah.

"As part of our celebration today," Sarah continued, "we have a fantastic Hulu contest with some incredible prizes up for grabs!" She paused for dramatic effect, and the crowd erupted in applause and cheers.

Kristol smiled as she watched the excitement ripple through the gathering. Sarah had a way of making even the simplest announcements feel like grand revelations.

Sarah went on to explain the rules of the contest and the prizes that were at stake, including Hulu gift cards, streaming devices, and even a trip to Hawaii for the lucky winner, airfare not included. The crowd's enthusiasm grew with each prize description, and anticipation was in the air. Sarah invited those who wanted to participate up to the stage. Twenty enthusiastic participants eagerly stepped forward, ready to showcase their hula skills in front of their colleagues.

"But that's not all," Sarah added with a mischievous grin, looking at the contestants. "We have a surprise twist to this contest. To enter, you'll need to show off your best hula hoop moves! That's right, folks, it's time to channel your inner Hawaiian spirit and get your hula hoop on!" Just then, Hula Hoops were brought out onto the stage.

Laughter and excitement filled the park as employees contemplated the challenge. It was a fun and unexpected twist to the contest, and everyone seemed enthusiastic to participate.

Sarah wrapped up her announcement by inviting the judges and everyone to have a blast. She reminded them that the winners would be announced afterward, adding an extra layer of fun and playfulness.

"Alright, folks, it's time to see who's got the best hula-hooping moves in the office!" Sarah exclaimed. "Our brave contestants are all set to give it their best shot."

With that, the lively Hawaiian music resumed, setting the perfect rhythm for the hula hoop competition. The contestants, each with a hula hoop in hand, began their spirited attempts to keep the hoops twirling around their waists.

Cheers and laughter erupted from the onlookers as they watched their coworkers spin, sway, and shimmy with the hoops. Some demonstrated impressive skills, while others found themselves in delightful and amusing hula mishaps.

As the competition heated up, Sarah and a few colleagues joined in the fun, showing off their hula-hooping talents and adding to the festive atmosphere.

The judges tallied the scores and announced the winners. The top three contestants, with the most impressive hula hooping skills, were awarded their prizes amidst cheers and applause from the crowd as the evening ended.

Chapter Eleven

IN SEARCH OF ANSWERS

Kristol couldn't shake the questions that had been troubling her. The flower district was her first destination as she hurried through the city streets. She needed to find Citta and get answers to unravel the mysteries that had stirred her soul. How could Citta be at the barbecue and not be at the barbecue at the same time?

As she approached the flower district, Kristol's pace quickened with anticipation. The flowers greeted her, but she had no time to savor their beauty today. She had a mission, and it was burning within her like a relentless flame.

Kristol navigated through the winding pathways lined with flower stalls, her eyes scanning for any sign of Citta. She couldn't forget Citta's words about the two sides of the coin, about fear and happiness being opposite but coexisting. She needed to grasp the deep insight behind those words.

She raced through the arching trees of Isa's flower stand, looking frantically for Citta. After what felt like an eternity, Kristol finally spotted Citta tucked away in a quiet corner. Citta was arranging bouquets with a smile on her face as if she had been expecting Kristol.

Determined and impatient, Kristol approached Citta, her voice firm. "Citta, we need to talk. I need some answers."

Citta stayed focused on her work, her eyes holding that depth of knowing Kristol had seen before. She nodded, indicating Kristol to sit on a nearby wooden bench. "Of course, Kristol," as if Citta was expecting this interaction.

"Citta, how is it that you were at the Hawaiian barbecue with my office party and then disappeared at the same time?" Kristol demanded.

Citta simply smiled, remaining silent as if the question held no significance in the grand scheme of things while tending to the flowers.

Kristol realized she wasn't going to get an answer to her question. With a resigned sigh, she continued, "You spoke about the two sides of the coin, about fear and happiness coexisting. Can you explain what you mean by that?"

Citta smiled gently and gestured to the flowers around them. "Look at these flowers, Kristol. Each one has its unique beauty, and they come in various colors and shapes. Some are bold and vibrant, while others are delicate and subtle. Now, consider the two sides of a coin. They are opposite, like fear and happiness, but they both exist within the same reality."

Kristol squinted, trying to grasp the concept. "But how can fear and happiness coexist? They seem so contradictory."

Citta nodded thoughtfully. "It's all about perception. Think of fear as the shadow side of happiness. Just as every flower has its shadow when the sun is shining, so does happiness, and its counterpart is fear. It's not about denying fear or pushing it away; it's about acknowledging its existence and understanding that it's part of the same whole."

Kristol leaned in, captivated by Citta's words. "So, you're saying that fear is not the opposite of happiness but rather a part of it?"

Citta smiled warmly. "When you accept that fear is a part of the same coin as happiness, you can transform it. You can learn from it, use it as a catalyst for growth, and ultimately find your way back to happiness. It's all about balance and embracing both sides of the coin."

As Kristol listened, she felt a bit of understanding and yet confused. Citta noticed her perplexed expression and decided to illustrate the concept with a touch of humor.

Citta chuckled, her eyes twinkling with mischief. "Imagine that life is like a game of musical chairs. We often find ourselves so engrossed in the competition for a chair that we forget to dance to the music. The music, the joy of the dance itself, is where the real magic resides. It's as if we're so focused on the result, we forget to enjoy the moment."

Slowly, a glimmer of understanding began to shine in her eyes. Her lips curled into a thoughtful smile, and her posture relaxed, signaling that the pieces of the puzzle were falling into place.

Citta nodded with a gentle smile. "You're getting it, Kristol. Both paradigms exist simultaneously. Life is like playing musical chairs, and the choice is yours – which one do you want to focus on? Do you want to be so fixated on the competition for a chair because you fear missing out and forget to dance to the music, or do you want to savor the dance itself, finding joy in every moment, regardless of the outcome?"

Kristol's eyes brightened with understanding. "I see it now. It's about shifting my perspective and choosing to embrace the joy in every moment rather than getting caught up in the race for the chair."

Citta nodded approvingly. "Happiness isn't just about reaching a destination; it's about finding joy in the journey. It's up to us to decide where we place our focus. When you choose to embrace the joy of the dance, you'll find that happiness is always within your reach, no matter the circumstances."

Citta's continued to share her knowledge with Kristol. "You see, it's the Law of Vibration. Everything in the universe is in a constant state of vibration, emitting its unique frequency. And emotions, well, they are no exception."

She extended her hand, drawing an imaginary scale in the air. "Imagine a scale from the lowest vibration, which is fear, all the way up to the highest vibration, which is pure joy and happiness. Every emotion we experience falls somewhere on this scale."

Kristol leaned in, captivated by Citta's explanation.

Citta continued, "Fear, anxiety, and doubt are on the lower end of the scale. They vibrate at a slower frequency and can feel heavy and constricting. But as we move up the scale, we encounter emotions like contentment, hope, and eventually, joy and happiness – even love."

She smiled warmly at Kristol. "Now, here's the beautiful part. Just like a radio dial, we have the power to tune into different frequencies. When you're feeling fear or any lower-vibrational emotion, it's like tuning into a station that plays dark and heavy music. But you can always turn the dial and choose to tune into a higher frequency, where joy and happiness are playing."

Kristol nodded, beginning to grasp the concept. "So, you're saying that happiness is just a higher frequency on the scale of emotions, and I can tune into it?"

Citta's eyes twinkled with approval. "Exactly! It's a matter of shifting your focus and intention. When you consciously choose thoughts and feelings that align with joy and gratitude, you raise your vibration and attract more positive experiences into your life."

Kristol took a moment to absorb this insight. It was a realization that happiness was not some elusive destination but a state of being that she could access at any moment.

Citta continued, "And here's the magic. When you consistently raise your vibration to the frequency of joy, you become a magnet for abundance, opportunities, and the things that bring you happiness. It's like attracting the right station with the most beautiful music."

Kristol felt a surge of hope and excitement. "So, by choosing happiness, I can also attract more abundance and fulfillment into my life?"

Citta nodded with a knowing smile. "Absolutely. The Law of Vibration is a universal principle, and it's always at work. When you align your thoughts, feelings, and actions with the higher frequencies of joy and gratitude, you'll find that your life begins to transform in remarkable ways."

Kristol took a deep breath, feeling more empowered. She realized that she held the key to her own happiness and abundance by choosing to vibrate at a higher frequency.

Citta leaned closer to Kristol, "Now, there's another important aspect of the quarter, one that often goes unnoticed. It's the ridge that runs along the edge, connecting the two seemingly opposite sides." Citta continued, "You see, this ridge represents the balance, the harmony between the two sides. It's like the balancing point of a seesaw. When you find that sweet spot, that point of equilibrium, you can navigate between fear and happiness with grace."

Kristol nodded, beginning to understand Citta's words. "So, it's not about entirely eliminating fear or negative emotions but finding that balance?"

Citta smiled, her eyes reflecting the depth of her wisdom. "Life is a dance between the light and the shadow, between joy and fear. It's about learning to embrace both sides and finding the harmony within."

Kristol pressed further. "How can you co-exist equally in fear and happiness, balancing between the two?"

Citta regarded Kristol with a knowing smile. "Ah, I never said that balance meant equally coexisting. Balance is not about making them equal, for they are not always equal in magnitude. It's about finding the right proportion, the harmony that suits your own unique life."

Kristol, frustrated, was processing Citta's words. "So, it's not about fear and happiness being equal partners on the scale?"

Citta shook her head gently. "No, it's about understanding that both fear and happiness have their place in your life. Imagine the scale of emotions as a lever that you can move up or down. It's not a fixed point where one abruptly shifts into happiness from fear. Instead, they blend and coexist along the scale, like the colors of a rainbow."

Kristol nodded, intrigued by Citta's analogy. "So, where does fear shift into happiness?"

Citta smiled knowingly. "That's the beauty of it, my dear. There's no specific point because it's a continuous spectrum. Fear can gradually transform into happiness as you move the lever up the scale. The more happiness you invite into your life, the less space there is for fear to linger. It's not about eliminating fear; it's about diminishing its presence."

Kristol contemplated Citta's words, trying to grasp the concept. "So, it's like a dance between the two emotions?"

Citta nodded, "As you introduce more happiness into your thoughts, actions, and experiences, you'll notice that fear begins to take a step back. The more you immerse yourself in happiness, gratitude, and positive emotions, the more you'll naturally shift away from fear. It's about nurturing a mindset that resonates with the higher vibrations of joy and contentment."

Kristol was struggling with the idea that she needed to eliminate all fear and negativity from her life, which had felt like an impossible task. But now, she realized that it was about moving her vibration up higher on the scale.

Citta continued, "When you can stand on the ridge, you become a master of your own emotions. You can choose when to lean into the happiness, savoring its beauty, and when to acknowledge fear, learning from its lessons. It's a dance of conscious awareness." Citta placed a hand on Kristol's shoulder, her touch reassuring. "Remember, you have the power to find that balance within yourself. Embrace the ridge, and you'll navigate life's ups and downs with grace and wisdom."

"You see," Citta continued," the ridge on this quarter is the Law of Vibration. It represents the balance scale between the two seemingly opposite sides. Just as the ridge connects the heads and tails."

Kristol nodded, starting to grasp the connection between the ridge and the Law of Vibration. "So, it's about aligning our own vibration with the frequency of happiness?"

Citta smiled, acknowledging Kristol's understanding. "When you focus on raising your vibration to match that of happiness, you naturally find that balance. You become a conscious co-creator of your reality, attracting more joy and abundance into your life."

Kristol couldn't help but seek further wisdom. "Citta, I have a question about fear. You mentioned that fear can never be entirely eliminated, but why do we need fear?"

"Fear is a natural response designed to keep us safe in dangerous situations. It's the body's way of preparing for a fight or flight response. However, there are two types of fear we need to distinguish – conditioned fear and naturally occurring fear." Citta elaborated.

Kristol leaned in, eager to learn more. "What's the difference?"

Citta began to explain, her voice gentle yet authoritative. "Conditioned fear is the fear we acquire through our experiences and conditioning. It includes fears like the fear of missing out, fear of rejection, or fear of failure. These fears aren't necessarily linked to immediate physical danger and can keep us in a state of anxiety and stress."

Kristol nodded, recognizing those fears in her own life. "So, we want to eliminate conditioned fear?"

Citta clarified, "The goal is to bring balance within the scale, allowing the natural fear – like the fear experienced in an earthquake – to remain for our safety. We can't eliminate all fear because some of it, the natural fear, serves as a protective mechanism. However, by reducing or even eliminating the conditioned fear, we can achieve a state where fear no longer dominates our lives."

Kristol pondered Citta's words. "So, is it possible to eliminate the conditioned fear?"

Citta smiled warmly. "Yes, Kristol, it is. By shifting our focus toward happiness, gratitude, and positive emotions, we can significantly reduce conditioned fear. When our mindset resonates with higher vibrations, fear has less room to persist. It's a gradual process, but one that leads to a more joyful and fulfilling life."

Kristol marveled at the simplicity. She realized that she had the power to shift her own vibration, to find that sweet spot on the vibrational scale, just like balancing on the ridge of the quarter.

"Citta, can you share how we can eliminate the conditioned fear?"

Citta gazed at the vibrant flowers. With a peaceful smile, she slowly backed away from the conversation. "I have other blooms to tend to, but remember, I'm always here when you seek guidance."

Taking the hint from Citta, Kristol nodded. "Thank you for your insights, Citta. I appreciate everything and have a lot to consider."

As Kristol made her way out of the arching trees, she approached Isa, who had been quietly tending to her shop. "Isa," Kristol began, her voice filled with curiosity, "do you know Citta well? She's quite an intriguing person."

Isa smiled warmly at Kristol. "Oh, Citta is a unique old soul sharing her wisdom and insights with those who seek it. Her connection to people and the energy of this place is truly something special."

Kristol nodded thoughtfully. "I felt my perspective shift after speaking with her. It's as if she opened my eyes to a whole new way of seeing the world."

Chapter Twelve

SYNCHRONISTIC OPPORTUNITY

As the days that followed the barbecue unfolded, Sarah found herself receiving praise and compliments from colleagues and superiors alike. It seemed that everyone had thoroughly enjoyed the event, and Sarah's meticulous planning had not gone unnoticed. She was elated by the positive feedback and felt a tremendous sense of accomplishment.

The executives had been particularly impressed with how smoothly the event had gone. They were delighted to see their employees so relaxed and having a great time. It was clear that the Hawaiian barbecue had boosted morale and fostered a sense of camaraderie among the staff.

As Sarah was going about her tasks in the office, Matt Anderson, one of the senior executives, approached her with a smile. He extended his hand to shake Sarah's and congratulated her on a job well done.

"Sarah," he began, "I must say that the Hawaiian barbecue was a tremendous success. You truly outdid yourself, and I wanted to express my gratitude for your hard work and dedication."

Sarah blushed with gratitude and replied, "Thank you, Mr. Anderson. I'm so glad everyone enjoyed it. It was a pleasure to plan and execute."

Matt Anderson nodded and continued, "Well, Sarah, I have another proposition for you. We've been so impressed with your organizational skills and creativity that we'd like to ask if you'd be interested in planning the company's Christmas party later this year."

Sarah's eyes widened with surprise and excitement. Planning the company's Christmas party was a significant responsibility, and it was an opportunity she hadn't expected. She took a moment to collect herself and replied, "I'd be honored, Mr. Anderson. I'd love to take on that challenge."

Mr. Anderson smiled and said, "Excellent! I do not doubt that you'll make it a memorable event, just like you did with the barbecue. We'll give you all the support you need to make it a success."

As Sarah walked away from the conversation, her heart was filled with anticipation and a sense of purpose. Planning the Christmas party was a big step forward in her career, and she was determined to make it as unforgettable as the Hawaiian barbecue.

Sarah rushed over to Kristol, her face radiant with excitement. "Kristol, you won't believe it! Matt Anderson just asked me to plan the Christmas Party this year!"

Kristol's eyes lit up, and she gave Sarah a warm hug. "That's fantastic news, Sarah! Congratulations! You're going to do an amazing job."

Sarah beamed at the praise, her enthusiasm bubbling over. "I'm so thrilled! This is a fantastic opportunity, and I can't wait to start planning. It's going to be the best Christmas Party our company has ever seen!"

As Sarah continued to share her plans and ideas for the upcoming Christmas Party, Kristol couldn't help but feel joy for her friend's success while simultaneously feeling a growing sense of internal distraction. Her mind wandered to her financial reality, where she had faced financial obligations, mounting hospital bills, and relentless creditors.

"Kristol, are you okay?" Sarah asked, noticing Kristol's distant expression.

Kristol snapped back to the present. "Oh, sorry, Sarah. I was just lost in thought for a moment. Please tell me more about your plans for the Christmas Party. I'm all ears."

Sarah continued to discuss her ideas excitedly, and Kristol listened attentively, offering suggestions and encouragement. However, beneath the surface, her mind was still drawn to her financial situation, even her conversation with Citta, and the balance between fear and happiness.

Seth entered Kristol's office with a warm smile, joining the conversation just as Sarah was sharing her excitement about planning the Christmas Party.

"Sarah, I heard the great news!" Seth exclaimed, clapping his hands in approval. "I'm sure you'll do an outstanding job."

Sarah grinned at the compliments, but as the conversation continued, Kristol's thoughts once again turned to her financial concerns. She couldn't help but ask the question that had been nagging at her. "Sarah, I don't mean to rain on your parade, but planning the Christmas Party is a significant task. It'll require a lot of time and effort. Did they offer you any additional compensation for taking on this responsibility? I mean, it's a big job, and it's not like they're giving you extra hours in the day."

Sarah's smile wavered slightly, and she nodded in understanding. "I appreciate your concern, Kristol. They didn't offer any extra pay, but I saw this as an opportunity to showcase my skills and make a positive impression on the executives. Besides, it's for the team, and I enjoy planning events."

Kristol nodded, but her concern persisted. "I get that, Sarah, and I admire your dedication. But we also have our daily work to manage, and you're putting a lot on your plate. Can you afford to spend that much time on party planning without it affecting your regular responsibilities?"

Sarah's expression became thoughtful as she considered Kristol's point. "You know, you're right. It will be a balancing act, and I might need to put in extra hours. But I'm up for the challenge, and I believe it'll all work out. Maybe I will put together a small team to assist." Sarah winked.

Seth chimed in, offering his support. "Sarah, if you need any assistance or if things get overwhelming, don't hesitate to reach out. Kristol and I can "team assist" you however we can."

Kristol smiled, appreciating the unity of her friends. "That's true, Sarah. We're here to support you in any way we can. Just remember to take care of yourself too. We've got your back."

As Kristol left the office that evening, her thoughts were all jumbled. Sarah's excitement about planning the Christmas Party was high-spirited, and Kristol was genuinely happy about her friend's opportunity. However, beneath her outward support, a persistent question lingered in her mind.

Citta's teachings left an impression on Kristol, but the idea of altogether eliminating conditioned fear had her intrigued, and Citta was not ready to impart that wisdom.

Kristol couldn't help but wonder if her financial worries were somehow tied to this conditioned fear.

The fear of failure was a prominent one; it had driven Kristol to strive for perfection in her corporate career, constantly pushing herself to excel. Yet, despite her efforts, Kristol often felt unrecognized and undervalued, leading to a persistent sense of stress and anxiety that had become part of everyday life.

There was the fear of disappointing others, especially her family and colleagues. She had always been the reliable one, the person everyone counted on. The weight of those expectations had compelled her to shoulder enormous responsibilities, sometimes at the expense of her own well-being. It was as if she feared letting others down, especially her mother and sister.

Lastly, the fear of not measuring up haunted her, pushing Kristol to seek validation and success constantly. She had set high standards for herself, and anything less felt like a failure. This fear had driven her to achieve, but it had also taken a toll on her emotional well-being.

As Kristol walked toward her car, she couldn't shake the feeling that these conditioned fears were somehow linked to her subconscious beliefs about money, success, and self-worth. The uncertainty weighed on her, dragging her down to a dark place of doom and dread.

Her encounter with Citta had left her with more questions than answers. Why hadn't Citta been ready to impart the wisdom on how to change these conditioned fears? What was she holding back? Kristol's mind raced with apprehension.

It was as if she had ventured into the depths of her psyche only to be frozen in fear. The darkness closed in around her, and the weight of her emotions felt like an anchor pulling her deeper into the ocean.

Kristol sat in her car, the engine idling, but she couldn't bring herself to drive. The dread had taken hold, and the thoughts of these conditioned fears paralyzed her. She needed answers, anything to break free from this grip of darkness.

A sudden, sharp rap on the window startled Kristol. She jumped in her seat, her heart racing from the unexpected intrusion. As she turned her head to see who was outside her car, she was met with the reassuring sight of Seth standing next to her window.

Rolling down the window, she quickly composed herself. "Seth, you scared me there for a moment."

Seth, noticing Kristol's expression, leaned in slightly and asked, "Hey, Kristol, everything ok?"

Kristol blinked, momentarily pulled from her thoughts, and replied, "Oh, sorry, Seth. I was just lost in thought. I'll be fine."

Seth peered at her with a concerned expression. "Are you sure? You looked pretty shaken up for someone who's just lost in thought."

Kristol sighed, realizing that her emotional turmoil must have been evident. She decided to confide in Seth, at least to some extent. "I've been thinking about some things, Seth. About the fears we carry, especially the conditioned ones. It's been bothering me."

Seth leaned against the car. "Fears, huh? Well, that's a deep topic. Anything in particular you want to talk about?"

"No, not really," Kristol replied with worry. "I just wish I knew how to let go of those fears that seem to control my life."

Seth, offering a reassuring smile, sensed Kristol's desire for solitude and gave her a reassuring nod. "No problem, Kristol. If you ever want to talk or need anything, I'm just a call or a chat away. Take your time."

Kristol managed a faint smile, grateful for Seth's understanding. "Thanks, Seth. I appreciate it."

Seth patted the roof of her car gently. "Anytime, Kristol." With those words, Seth finally walked away, leaving Kristol to her contemplations and the quiet solitude of her car.

Kristol arrived home, happy to be in the familiar energy of her condo. As she stepped inside, Max and Bella came running into the room, greeting her. Kristol made her way to the kitchen table, her purse slung over her shoulder. The weight of the day bore down on her, and she felt the urge to unpack her purse, both literally and metaphorically. With a sigh, she began to empty its contents onto the table, scattering the items in a haphazard pile.

Among the jumble of objects, she came across the prescription slip the doctor had given her earlier for the anxiety that lurked inside of her. Part of her longed for the relief the medication could bring, especially from these panic attacks. But another part hesitated, recognizing that masking the symptoms wouldn't address the root causes.

As she contemplated her choices, her fingers brushed up against a folded piece of paper that was tucked away in a corner of her purse. She retrieved it, unfolding the flyer she was given at the winery – an opportunity to escape the demands of daily life.

The timing felt serendipitous. The retreat, spanning over a week, promised healing, self-discovery, and personal growth. Nestled in the heart of a tranquil nature setting, the retreat center was a sanctuary of serenity and peace.

Each day of the retreat was thoughtfully structured to provide a holistic healing experience. Mornings began with guided meditation sessions, allowing participants to center themselves and cultivate mindfulness. These moments of introspection set the tone for the day ahead.

The retreat offered a rich variety of healing activities, catering to different aspects of well-being. Yoga sessions provided physical rejuvenation and inner balance, while nature walks and outdoor excursions allowed participants to connect with the natural world and find solace in its beauty.

Instructional workshops talked about the power of emotions and their impact on perception and reality. Expert facilitators guided participants through discussions and exercises, helping them understand the intricate interplay between their emotional states and the way they viewed the world.

In the afternoons, the retreat provided ample time for personal reflection and introspection. Participants were encouraged to journal, meditate, or find a quiet space to contemplate their journey, and this sacred time allowed them to process their experiences and insights, fostering deeper self-awareness.

Evenings were reserved for communal gatherings, where participants shared their learnings and revelations. It was a space for connection, support, and the celebration of newfound wisdom. Fireside chats and group discussions often led to profound conversations that enriched the retreat experience.

As Kristol carefully examined the flyer for the retreat, her fingers traced the details that would shape her journey of self-discovery. The dates were rapidly approaching. She realized this was the "something different" she had yearned for in her life this summer.

The pricing for the retreat was within her budget, considering her current financial situation and the value it promised in terms of personal growth and healing was priceless. Kristol recognized that this was a synchronistic moment, something that had been happening more and more to her, and she was determined to seize it.

Kristol decided to take action. She reached for her laptop and clicked on the retreat's website, where she found the registration page. As Kristol filled out the form, she couldn't help but feel a sense of liberation and anticipation. It was a step towards a new beginning, an opportunity to embrace the happiness she so deeply desired.

After confirming her registration and making the necessary arrangements, Kristol leaned back in her chair, a smile of determination on her face. The retreat was coming up soon, and it was a step closer to a version of herself she had longed to become.

Kristol's excitement had reached new heights as she prepared for the upcoming retreat. With her dogs, forgetting about dinner, she headed to the park with a sense of freedom that seemed to course through her veins.

The sun hung low in the sky, casting a warm, golden hue over the park. Children played on swings, dogs chased after tennis balls, and the laughter of families filled the air. Max and Bella wasted no time in joining the joyful chaos, their tails wagging and their spirits high.

Kristol, walking without her brace for the first time in what felt like ages, felt an incredible lightness in her step. She laughed as she chased after her furry companions, the worries and stresses of her everyday life fading into the background.

As she rounded a corner of the park, she nearly collided with Liam, who was standing near a park bench, watching his own dog frolic and play.

"Kristol, you seem to be bursting with energy today," Liam remarked as he stood up to greet her.

Kristol grinned, her eyes shining with enthusiasm. "Oh, Liam, you have no idea! I've registered for a retreat, and I can't contain my excitement. It's like a whole new world is opening up to me."

Liam raised an eyebrow, genuinely intrigued. "A retreat? That sounds amazing. What is it about?"

And tell him she did. Kristol launched into an animated monologue about the retreat, describing the week-long experience filled with healing activities, introspection, and instruction on the power of emotions. She spoke of the beautiful setting, the opportunity for personal growth, and the chance to connect with like-minded individuals seeking transformation.

Liam listened with rapt attention, his head spinning and a genuine smile playing on his lips as he absorbed Kristol's exuberance. Her new zest for life and her determination to embrace new experiences resonated with him.

Liam began, "It's inspiring to see your passion for this retreat. It's clear that you're ready to embrace this with an open heart and a free spirit."

Kristol's eyes sparkled with excitement. "I am, Liam. I feel like this is precisely what I need right now – a chance to step out of my comfort zone and explore."

As the conversation continued, Kristol's enthusiasm remained undiminished. She talked about her plans for the retreat, the healing activities she looked forward to, and the sense of freedom she hoped to achieve. And then, almost impulsively, she turned to Liam with a request.

"You know, I'll need someone to take care of Max and Bella while I'm away," Kristol said with a hopeful look. "Would you be willing to look after them? I trust you, and I know they'll be in good hands."

Liam didn't hesitate to agree. "Of course, Kristol. I'd be happy to take care of them for you."

Kristol's face lit up with gratitude. "Thank you, Liam. I knew I could count on you." Throwing her arms around him, giving Liam a big hug.

Chapter Thirteen

COUNTDOWN TO TRANSFORMATION

Kristol's excitement about the upcoming retreat seemed to radiate from her as she arrived at work early the following day. She couldn't contain her enthusiasm, and it didn't go unnoticed by her colleagues, including Seth.

Seth, curious about his coworker's uncharacteristic energy, decided to investigate. He strolled over to Kristol's office as he took in her enthusiasm.

"Kristol, you're practically glowing this morning," Seth remarked with a bemused smile. "You seem pretty excited, definitely a little different than when you left last night."

Kristol offered a warm smile while deciding to keep some details to herself. "Oh, just something different, Seth. It's an opportunity I've been looking forward to."

Seth leaned against the edge of her desk, clearly intrigued. "Something different, huh? Sounds mysterious; care to share more?"

Kristol decided to provide a little insight without revealing too much. "Well, it's a retreat. It's a chance for me to explore some new experiences."

Seth nodded, respecting her desire for privacy, but at the same time, ever curious, "I'm happy for you. I won't pry, but when is this retreat? Where is it? How long will you be gone? What kind of stuff are you going to be doing there?"

Kristol couldn't help but laugh, aware of Seth's strong tendency for office gossip. She replied, "Well, it's going to be a little over a week, and there's a whole range of activities planned. It's a mix of introspection, instruction, and, you know, a chance to explore some interesting concepts."

Seth, clearly wanting to know more, chose to respect her desire to keep things under wraps. "Sounds like it's going to be quite the adventure. I hope you have a fantastic time, Kristol."

Kristol nodded appreciatively. "Thank you, Seth. I'll make sure to bring back some stories to share."

Kristol settled into her work for the morning, her mind a whirlwind of anticipation for the upcoming retreat. As the clock ticked closer to noon, she couldn't help but feel her excitement build.

With her tasks for the morning neatly organized, Kristol started her day. She exchanged a few brief pleasantries with her colleagues, mostly keeping her plans to herself. It was almost lunchtime, and she had a list of things to do before leaving work for the day.

As the clock struck noon, Kristol wasted no time. She swiftly gathered her things and made her way to the office exit. She was determined, and nothing was going to stand in her way. Seth was quick to notice Kristol's hasty departure. He jumped up from his desk and hurried to catch her before she could slip away.

"Kristol, hold on a second!" he called out, catching up to her just as she reached the door. "Where are you off to in such a hurry?"

Kristol, not wanting to reveal too much, flashed Seth a friendly smile but kept her response vague. "Oh, just some errands I need to take care of, Seth. Nothing too exciting."

Seth's persisted. "Errands? It must be something important for you to leave work in such a rush. Care to share the details?" he probed.

Kristol chuckled, trying to deflect his inquiries. "You know how it is, Seth. Sometimes, life throws a few surprises our way, and we have to go with the flow. I'll catch up with you later, okay?"

With that, Kristol made a hasty exit, leaving Seth with more questions than answers. She had a date with destiny, and she wasn't about to let anyone or anything stand in her way.

As Kristol hurried through the office corridors, her thoughts preoccupied with the upcoming retreat, she barely noticed the people around her. Her pace was swift, her confidence unwavering. She was so focused that she almost collided with a man stepping out of the elevator.

"Whoa, watch your step there," the man chuckled, extending a hand to steady her. It was Benjamin, the same gentleman she had literally bumped into at the Hawaiian barbecue.

Kristol blinked in surprise, recognizing his face instantly. "Benjamin, I'm so sorry," she exclaimed, feeling slightly embarrassed by the encounter.

Benjamin smiled warmly, his eyes crinkling at the corners. "No harm done. It seems we have a talent for running into each other, don't we?"

Kristol smiled bashfully; her tension momentarily eased by his friendly demeanor. "It does seem that way. I guess I'm in a bit of a hurry today."

Benjamin grinned, acknowledging Kristol's comment. "I can tell, Kristol. Sometimes life has a way of keeping us on our toes, doesn't it?"

Kristol turned towards Benjamin with a curious expression. "Are you here in the office today?"

Benjamin nodded, his demeanor shifting to a more business-like tone. "Yes, I am. We have a meeting with the team to discuss some work-related projects."

Kristol was intrigued by the mention of work. "Ah, I see. Well, I won't keep you then. Good luck with your meeting."

Benjamin smiled appreciatively. "Thank you, Kristol. Maybe we will run into each other again soon." The elevator returned, and the doors slid open, and Kristol stepped inside, exchanging friendly goodbyes.

Kristol quickly raced to the flower district to share her exciting news with Citta. She couldn't wait to tell her about the upcoming retreat and the positive changes she hoped to bring into her life. She also had questions from their last conversation that she wanted cleared up before she went on the retreat.

As she entered the flower shop and ducked under the arching trees, Kristol expected to find Citta tending to her vibrant blooms as usual. However, to her disappointment, Citta was nowhere to be found. The flower stand, usually full of wisdom and guidance, stood empty, with its fragrant blooms offering no consolation.

Kristol's enthusiasm began to deflate like a balloon losing air. She had been so eager to share her newfound path to self-discovery and transformation with Citta, hoping for guidance and support. Now, faced with an empty shop, she felt abandoned and confused.

She stood in the middle of the shop, the weight of her expectations pressing down on her. It was as if the world had shifted, leaving her alone in a place that once felt like a bridge between two realms. Kristol couldn't help but wonder why Citta had chosen this moment to be absent, and she struggled to contain her disappointment.

Isa, with her gentle smile and warm presence, walked up and stood beside Kristol, greeting her in a soothing tone. "Hello, dear Kristol. Is everything alright? You seem a bit perplexed."

Kristol sighed, her confusion still evident. "Isa, I don't know what happened. I came here to see Citta, but she's nowhere to be found. It's just... unexpected."

Isa placed a comforting hand on Kristol's shoulder. "Sometimes, my dear, even those who offer guidance need their moments of rest and reflection. Citta may have her reasons for being absent today."

Kristol nodded, appreciating Isa's wisdom. "You're right, Isa. I guess I was just so eager to share my news with her. This retreat means a lot to me, and I wanted her guidance."

Isa's eyes held a knowing sparkle. "The journey to self-discovery can sometimes be a solitary one, but it's in those moments of solitude that we often find our most authentic insights. Citta will be here when the time is right."

Kristol smiled, feeling reassured by Isa's words. "Thank you, Isa. You always have a way of bringing clarity to my thoughts."

Isa's smile deepened. "It's my pleasure, dear Kristol. Remember, the path to self-discovery is a journey worth taking, even if it means walking it alone for a little while."

With Isa's words echoing in her mind, Kristol took a deep breath and left the flower district. On the way home, she stopped by the grocery store and ran other errands.

As Kristol busied herself with preparations for the upcoming retreat, her phone buzzed, and she saw her sister Emily's name flashing on the screen. She answered the call with a smile, expecting their usual friendly banter.

"Hey there, Emily! What's up?" Kristol greeted her sister cheerfully.

Emily's voice on the other end sounded somewhat perturbed. "Kristol, I just wanted to remind you about our tennis match this weekend."

Kristol froze for a moment, her heart sinking as she realized that in all the excitement and anticipation of the retreat, she had forgotten entirely about her prior commitments, including the tennis match she had planned with Emily.

"Oh, Emily, I'm so sorry," Kristol began apologetically. "I completely forgot about it. Something important came up, and I won't be able to make it this weekend."

There was a moment of silence on the other end, followed by a sigh from Emily. "Kristol, you're always so wrapped up in your work, and now whatever this 'important' thing is. I wish you'd make more time for your family."

Kristol could sense the jealousy and frustration in her sister's voice, feeling a pang of guilt. Being dedicated to her career often meant it was at the expense of her family and personal time, a pattern she was attempting to break. It seems as if she had inadvertently hurt her sister in the process.

"I know, Emily, and I'm truly sorry," Kristol replied sincerely. "I promise we'll reschedule our tennis match when I get back, and I'll make an effort to spend more time with the family."

Emily's tone softened, but still sulking, and she said, "I appreciate that, Kristol. Just remember that family is important too."

Kristol hesitated for a moment before responding, "Emily, the reason I won't be able to make it this weekend is that I'll be out of town."

"Out of town? For what?" Emily asked.

Kristol took a deep breath, deciding it was best to be honest with her sister. "I'm attending a retreat," she admitted. "It's something I've been wanting to do for a while. A chance to step away from work, clear my mind, and focus on personal growth and well-being."

There was a brief pause on the other end of the line, and then Emily replied, "A retreat? That sounds interesting. What kind of retreat is it?"

Kristol smiled, relieved that her sister seemed more intrigued than upset. "It's a week-long retreat focused on self-discovery, mindfulness, and healing. I think it's exactly what I need right now."

Emily's tone became more supportive as she said, "Well, if it's something that will help you, then I'm all for it. Just promise me you'll take some time to relax and enjoy yourself."

Kristol nodded, even though Emily couldn't see her. "I promise, Emily. I'll make the most of this opportunity, and we'll plan something fun together when I get back."

Emily seemed to be more understanding now, and Kristol felt a sense of relief. She had expected a bit of resistance from her family, but Emily's unexpected acceptance made her decision to attend the retreat feel even more fitting.

"Thanks, Kristol," Emily said sincerely. "I hope you have a fantastic time at your retreat, and I can't wait to hear all about it when you return."

Kristol smiled, grateful for her sister's understanding. "I'll definitely share everything with you when I'm back. Thanks for being so understanding, Emily."

As Kristol lay in her bed that night, her mind was filled with anticipation. She couldn't help but think about all the last-minute preparations she needed to make before leaving for the week-long journey.

One of the most critical arrangements was for her beloved dogs, Max and Bella. Kristol had asked her friend, Liam, to take care of them while she was away. Liam had agreed without hesitation, and it was a relief to know that her furry companions would be in good hands. However, as she lay there in the quiet of her room, doubts and worries crept in.

"What if Max and Bella give Liam a hard time?" Kristol wondered aloud. She knew that her dogs could be a handful, and she didn't want to burden her friend with their care. But Liam had reassured her that he was up for the task.

Kristol mentally went through a checklist of things she needed to leave for Liam – their food, toys, and a list of their daily routines.

She wanted to make sure he had everything he needed to make their stay as comfortable as possible.

Aside from the logistics of her trip, Kristol's mind wandered to what lay ahead at the retreat. She had read about the various activities and workshops that were planned – meditation sessions, group discussions, and even a course on the power of emotions. It all sounded fascinating and slightly intimidating at the same time.

"What am I getting myself into?" Kristol mused. The idea of delving deep into her emotions and exploring her inner world was starting to feel nerve-wracking. She knew that personal growth often came with moments of discomfort, but she was determined to embrace the experience.

As the night wore on, Kristol continued to make mental notes about what she needed to pack and the tasks she needed to complete in the morning. She couldn't help but feel excitement and trepidation about the retreat that awaited her. But beneath it all, there was a sense of hope and anticipation – a feeling that this retreat could be the answers she had been searching for in her life.

Chapter Fourteen

EXPLORING THE MIND-BODY CONNECTION

The morning sun rays beamed over Kristol's living room as she made the final preparations for her retreat. She had carefully finalized her bags with essentials, including comfortable clothing, a journal, and a sense of anticipation for the journey ahead.

As she double-checked her packing list, the sound of a car pulling into her driveway caught her attention. She knew it was Liam arriving to take care of Max and Bella during her absence. The dogs, Max and Bella, who were usually full of energy, sensed a change in the air and watched with curious eyes as Liam approached with his dog.

Kristol opened the door to greet him, a smile on her face. "Hey, Liam! Thanks so much for helping out with the dogs. I really appreciate it."

Liam returned her smile warmly. "No problem at all, Kristol. Max and Bella are great company, and it'll be good practice for me. Plus, I could use a little break from my usual routine."

They exchanged pleasantries as Liam made himself comfortable in her living room, and Kristol gathered Max and Bella's belongings. She had prepared a detailed list of their daily routines, feeding schedules, and even their favorite toys. She wanted to make sure that Liam had everything he needed to keep the dogs happy and comfortable.

"Here you go," Kristol said, handing him the list and a bag filled with Max and Bella's essentials. "I've also left some emergency contact numbers in case anything comes up."

Liam nodded, appreciating her thoroughness. "You've thought of everything, Kristol. Don't worry; I'll take good care of them. You go and enjoy your retreat."

With a final pat on Max and Bella's heads, Kristol bid her dogs farewell, her heart filled with excitement for her adventure.

As she made her way to her car with her packed bags, Liam called out to her, "Hey, Kristol, before you go, just remember to stay open to whatever comes your way at that retreat. Sometimes, the unexpected can be the most transformative."

Kristol turned to him, a thoughtful expression on her face. "Thanks, Liam. I'll keep that in mind. See you in a week!" With a wave, she got into her car and drove away, leaving her home and her everyday life behind.

It was a six-hour drive to the retreat center that stretched ahead of Kristol like an uncharted path into the unknown. She had programmed the center's address into her GPS, and the soothing voice guided her through the scenic countryside. The road stretched endlessly, winding through lush forests and open fields, each passing mile bringing her closer to her destination.

Kristol found relaxation in long drives, the rhythmic hum of the engine, and the changing landscapes, allowing her thoughts to wander freely. As she drove, she reflected on the choices that had led her to this moment – the decision to take a step back from her demanding career, the flyer at the winery, and the decision to go on this retreat alone.

The hours passed, and the sun hung high in the sky, casting rays through the car's windows. Kristol marveled at the beauty of the world outside her car – the rolling hills, the quaint little towns she passed through. It was a reminder of the world's vastness. Slowly, the scenery changed into a dry desert.

Around mid-afternoon, her GPS announced her arrival at the retreat center. Anticipation filled her as she turned onto a cactus-lined road that led to the entrance. Desert Ironwood, Mesquite trees, and large boulder rocks painted the surroundings in a majestic earth tone. The change of environment brought Kristol internal peace.

As she pulled up to the main building, she noticed a few other cars parked nearby. It appeared that some of the other retreat participants had already arrived. Kristol parked her car and took a moment to breathe in the dry air. She could feel the energy of the retreat.

With her bags, Kristol made her way into the main building, where a friendly staff member greeted her. They checked her in and provided her with a map of the center, along with some basic information about the schedule and activities. She was then directed to her room, which she would be sharing with a fellow retreat participant.

Upon entering the room, Kristol was greeted by her roommate, a warm and welcoming woman named Lori, who arrived about thirty minutes before Kristol. They exchanged introductions and quickly struck up a conversation, sharing their reasons for attending the retreat and their hopes for what lay ahead.

As the afternoon turned to evening, Kristol and Lori joined the other participants in the dining hall for a communal dinner. The atmosphere was filled with new friendships as people from all walks of life came together with a shared purpose – to explore the depths of their inner selves.

Kristol expressed gratitude for the path that had led her here. The retreat was a departure from her usual routine, a break from the demands of her corporate career. She was ready to embrace whatever experiences and lessons lay ahead, knowing that this retreat was "the something different" she had been yearning for.

The atmosphere at the round table buzzed with new connections and shared experiences. Lori and Kristol found themselves seated with two other women, Sophie and Emma, as well as two men,

James and David. The diverse group of participants represented a spectrum of ages, backgrounds, and life experiences. They all introduced themselves to each other.

Sophie, a cheerful woman with a warm smile, initiated the conversation. "So, what inspired each of you to come to this retreat?" she asked, directing her question to the group.

Kristol, feeling wholly open and vulnerable in this space, decided to share her thoughts first. "Well, for me, it's about seeking something different, you know? I've spent so much of my life focused on my career and external achievements, but I've always felt like there's more to explore within myself. This retreat felt like the perfect opportunity to find answers."

Lori nodded in agreement. "I can relate to that," she said. "I've been on a journey of self-discovery for a while now, and I thought this retreat would be a great way to deepen that exploration. Plus, the natural surroundings here are so inspiring."

James, a middle-aged man with a thoughtful demeanor, chimed in, "I've been dealing with stress and anxiety for years. I've tried therapy and medication, but I wanted to explore more holistic approaches to healing. I have doubt, but this retreat seemed like a promising avenue."

Emma, a younger, feisty woman, shared her perspective. "I've always been fascinated by the power of emotions and how they shape our lives. I'm here to gain a deeper understanding of that and hopefully find some tools to navigate life's ups and downs more gracefully."

David, a seasoned traveler who exuded a sense of calm, spoke next. "I've been to various retreats over the years, and each one has offered unique insights and growth. This time, I wanted to explore the concept of balance in my life."

The conversation flowed naturally as they shared their reasons for being at the retreat and their expectations for the days ahead. It became evident that, despite their different paths and backgrounds, they were all united by a common desire to discover the transformative power of their own emotions.

As the group settled into their dinner conversation, their enthusiastic exchange of ideas was interrupted by the warm presence of the retreat hosts. A man and a woman, both radiating a sense of tranquility and wisdom, stood at the front of the dining area. The participants fell into a hushed silence, turning their attention to the hosts.

The woman, whose name tag read "Elena," spoke first. Her voice was soothing, like a gentle breeze rustling through leaves. "Good evening, everyone," she began, her smile conveying a genuine sense of welcome. "We hope you're enjoying your first evening here at the retreat. We want to take a moment to officially welcome you and provide some information about the schedule for the coming days."

The man, introduced as "Daniel," continued, his presence exuding a sense of groundedness. "First, we'd like to emphasize that this retreat is about your personal journey. While we have a structured schedule, everything is optional, but we encourage you to attend the Power of Emotions instructional classes every day. Mostly, feel free to participate in any activities that resonate with you. If you need time for introspection or simply to rest, that's absolutely encouraged as well."

Elena chimed in, "That being said, we have some wonderful offerings lined up for you. Each day of this retreat will focus on a different aspect of the power of emotions—how they affect us mentally, physically, financially, and spiritually."

Daniel added, "Tomorrow, we'll begin with the mental effects of emotions. Our instruction classes will help you understand how emotions influence your thoughts and cognitive processes. You'll gain valuable insights into managing your mind."

Elena continued, "On the following day, we will cover the physical effects of emotions. We'll explore practices like yoga and meditation each day to help you connect with the sensations in your body, as well as physical 'dis-ease' created by emotions."

Elena's eyes sparkled as she shared, "We've also dedicated a day to the financial effects of emotions. It's a chance to examine your relationship with money and abundance. Many of our participants have found this day to be quite transformative in their financial lives."

Daniel nodded, "Then, we'll move on to the spiritual effects of emotions, a day focused on inner exploration and connection to your higher self, completing the retreat with a transformational experience. You'll have opportunities for reflection, meditation, and spiritual practices if you choose to participate."

The retreat hosts, Elena and Daniel, continued to address the eager participants, providing logistical details to ensure everyone felt comfortable and informed during their stay.

Elena smiled warmly and said, "We want to make your experience here as seamless as possible. To that end, please know that this retreat is all-inclusive. Your registration fee covers your accommodations, meals, and all activities."

Daniel chimed in, "We also have a lovely lounge area where you can relax, chat with fellow participants, or enjoy a cup of herbal tea whenever you like. Additionally, there's a no-host bar available if you wish to have alcoholic beverages during your stay. We encourage you to enjoy your time here in a way that feels right for you."

Elena added, "As for your personal schedules, you'll find them in your welcome packets. They include details about the activities, times, and locations for each day. If you have any questions or need assistance, our team is here to help. Don't hesitate to reach out."

As the retreat hosts concluded their welcome address, Kristol turned her attention back to the conversation at her table. Lori, her roommate, warmly smiled as she sipped on her herbal tea. The others around the table were engaged in discussing their expectations for the retreat.

Sophie, with her calming presence, leaned in and shared her thoughts. "I've been looking forward to this retreat for a while now. I'm hoping to find some inner peace and clarity, especially in my hectic life."

Kristol nodded in agreement. "I can relate to that. It's so easy to get caught up in the chaos of daily life and lose sight of what truly matters."

Lori shared her own perspective, "I think it's important to be in touch with our emotions. Sometimes, we suppress them, and it can have a negative impact on our well-being."

Kristol appreciated the openness and sincerity of the fellow participants. "You're all right; emotions play a significant role in our lives. I'm looking forward to gaining a deeper understanding of how to harness their power for positive change."

As their conversation gradually wound down, the participants at the table exchanged warm smiles and well-wishes. The day's travel had taken its toll, and everyone was eager to settle into their rooms for some much-needed rest.

Kristol bid her new friends goodnight and made her way to her room with Lori. The retreat center had a serene ambiance, with softly lit pathways leading to the accommodations. Their room was inviting, adorned with earthy tones and natural textures that complemented the surrounding desert.

Kristol and Lori exchanged a few friendly words as they prepared for bed, both feeling eager. As they settled into their respective beds, the night encased them in a gentle embrace, promising a restful sleep and the beginning of a transformative experience.

The next morning, 6:00 am came early. The sun was already shining brightly, and the temperatures were warming up. Kristol awoke, ready to start the day with the morning yoga class and meditation. Lori by her side, they quickly arrived at the yoga studio, where the day's activities were set to begin.

The yoga studio welcomed them with an atmosphere of serenity. Soft, soothing music played in the background, creating an ambiance of calmness. The large windows allowed the morning sunlight to filter in, casting a warm and gentle glow and a sweet smell of almond vanilla filling the room.

They found their designated spots on comfortable yoga mats arranged in a semi-circle. Around them, other participants settled in. The yoga instructor, a gentle-looking woman with big eyes and a calming presence stood at the front of the room. The class began with a few minutes of gentle stretching and deep, mindful breathing. Kristol closed her eyes and focused on her breath, letting go of any tension or thoughts that lingered from the previous day. With each inhalation and exhalation, she felt herself becoming more centered and present.

The instructor guided them through a series of yoga poses that focused on grounding, balance, and flexibility. The combination of yoga and deep breathing left Kristol feeling rejuvenated and centered, ready to embrace the day ahead.

After the yoga session, they transitioned seamlessly into a meditation practice. The yoga studio provided the perfect setting for quiet contemplation. The instructor led them through meditation exercises, helping them connect with their inner selves and cultivate a sense of peace.

Afterward, Kristol and Lori made their way to the dining hall for a healthy breakfast, nourishing their physical bodies. As they got prepared and ready for the day, they gathered their belongings. Heading over to the class, they mindlessly chattered about the anticipation of what they were going to learn.

Inside the classroom, they found their seats eager to learn about the world of emotions and their mental impact. At the front of the room, the instructor, Stuart, stood poised to guide them through this transformative experience.

Stuart initiated the class with a captivating introduction, carefully articulating the intentions for the day. His words emphasized the interactive and participatory nature of the class on the mental effects of emotions.

"Here, we believe in experiential learning." Stuart began. "We won't be merely passive recipients listening to lectures; we are going to roll up our sleeves and put theory into tangible practice." He continued, "Muscle testing, also known as applied kinesiology, is a fascinating technique that offers valuable insights into the interplay between our emotions and our physical well-being. At the heart of this method lies the concept that our thoughts and emotions emit energetic frequencies that can impact our physical and mental state."

Kristol was in awe, wondering how this all connected to what Citta had been teaching her.

Stuart continued his lecture, "The human body is surrounded by an electromagnetic energy field that reflects our mental and emotional condition. When we experience emotions like anger, this energy field can contract or weaken, leading to decreased physical strength. Conversely, higher emotions, such as love and joy, can expand and strengthen this energy field, enhancing our overall vitality."

Kristol absorbed valuable insights about how emotions can affect the mind. She learned about the influential power of thought patterns, explored the impact of emotions on decision-making processes, and acquired techniques to preserve mental equilibrium and clarity when confronted with the turbulence of intense emotional experiences.

Stuart transitioned seamlessly into a captivating demonstration of muscle testing. He scanned the faces in the room and raised his hand, signaling for a volunteer. Sophie, who had been engrossed in the previous discussion at dinner, enthusiastically raised her hand, ready to experience muscle testing firsthand. Stuart welcomed her to the front of the class.

He skillfully showcased how thoughts and emotions are energetic frequencies projected from the body and the subconscious mind. Furthermore, he shared how various emotional states could either elevate or diminish an individual's energy field.

Stuart demonstrated the technique by having one participant extend their arm horizontally while he gently applied downward pressure. This established a baseline strength for the individual. Then, he instructed the participant to think of a situation that invoked a lower emotional state, such as anger or sadness. As the participant focused on this emotion, Stuart repeated the arm pressure test. In most cases, the arm weakened and dropped, reflecting a decrease in the individual's energy field.

Then Stuart demonstrated the effect of positive emotions by having the participant think of a joyful or loving experience. Again, he repeated the arm pressure test, and in the majority of cases, the arm remained strong and stable. The change showcases how higher emotions can enhance the body's energy field, leading to increased physical strength.

The demonstration took an intriguing turn as Stuart engaged the audience to participate in the process fully. It was an illustration of the interconnectedness of thoughts, emotions, and the energetic vibrations they emitted.

He turned to the audience and explained, "Now, let's see how our collective thoughts and emotions can influence our volunteer, Sophie, here." He asked the audience to shout out various emotions, both positive and negative, for Sophie to experience. The participants in the audience enthusiastically called out emotions like joy, love, anger, fear, gratitude, and sadness.

With each emotion called out, Sophie experienced corresponding changes in their energy field and muscle response. When positive emotions were shouted, her energy field expanded, and her muscle test stayed strong. When negative emotions were called out, her energy field contracted, and her muscles weakened.

"What we have witnessed here today," Stuart shared, "Is a powerful illustration of the interconnectedness of our thoughts and emotions. It serves as a clear reminder that our emotional state is not isolated; it resonates with and can influence those around us. The negative, lower emotions we experienced had a noticeable impact on Sophie's energy field, causing a decrease in the energy field. The positive, higher emotions we collectively generated bolstered her energy field, enhancing her energy field."

Stuart continued, "This exercise demonstrates the significance of our internal emotional environment and the external environment we create without thoughts and feelings. It highlights the potential we hold to uplift ourselves and others through awareness and conscious intention. As we explore the effects of emotions on our mental and physical states further in this course, remember the power you possess to impact your life positively and also those around you."

Kristol found herself deeply engrossed in this experiential learning, profoundly grateful for the opportunity to not only grasp the theoretical underpinnings but also witness the tangible and transformative effects of emotions on the energetic realm. Stuart thanked Sophie for volunteering and actively participating in the demonstration, allowing everyone to witness the profound effects of emotions on our energy fields.

As the class continued, Stuart engaged the students in an interactive exercise. He encouraged everyone to pair up with a partner, and each person was to think of a specific emotion while their partner attempted to perform the muscle test.

Pairs across the room began to experiment, some thinking of joy, love, or gratitude while others focused on emotions like anger, fear, or sadness. They took turns performing the muscle test on their partners, noticing the distinct differences in the strength of the response. Laughter and amazement filled the room as participants realized the tangible impact of their emotional states on their physical bodies.

Stuart brought the class back from their exercise. "As you've experienced firsthand, our emotions are like signals broadcasting 24/7. Think of yourselves as these emotional radio towers, constantly emitting frequencies into the world. But remember, we're not just transmitters; we're also receivers. Our emotional frequencies are like antennas, tuned to pick up and interpret the signals from others and our environment.

Imagine your emotional state as the frequency you're tuned into. When you're in a state of joy, love, or gratitude, you're broadcasting and receiving those high-vibrational frequencies. But when you're in a state of anger, fear, or sadness, those lower frequencies dominate your transmission.

What we've learned today is that these emotional frequencies aren't confined to us; they extend beyond our bodies, affecting the energy fields of those around us. You have the power to influence the emotional states of the people you interact with daily.

It's essential to become aware of the emotional frequencies you're transmitting and receiving because they have a direct impact on your well-being and the well-being of those in your life. By becoming conscious of your emotional radio station, you can choose to tune into higher frequencies, fostering more positive experiences and relationships.

In the coming days, we'll uncover how these emotional frequencies affect various aspects of our lives, including our physical health and finances. Remember, you can adjust your emotional dial, enhancing the quality of your life and those around you." With that, Stuart concluded class.

Chapter Fifteen

CONFRONTING THE SHADOW WITHIN

During dinner, Kristol, Lori, Sophie, Emma, David, and James gathered at their table, ready to share their experiences and insights from the day's classes and activities.

Lori, completely upbeat, began, "I was really intrigued by the muscle testing demonstration. It was amazing to see how our thoughts and emotions can affect our energy fields and those of others. It made me realize just how important it is to be aware of our emotional state."

Kristol nodded in agreement, her own excitement evident. "Yes, and Stuart's explanation about us being like radio towers emitting signals 24/7 was eye-opening. It's incredible to think that we are constantly sending out emotional frequencies that can influence our well-being and the well-being of those around us."

Sophie, who had volunteered earlier for the demonstration, chimed in, "I felt the impact of the collective emotions of the audience during the demonstration. It was a powerful.

Sometimes, it felt like it could knock me over. We are so interconnected with everyone, our emotions truly create ripple effects."

James, who has been quietly listening, raised an eyebrow skeptically. "I get that it's fascinating, but how does all of this help with anxiety and stress? It was a bit too abstract for me."

Kristol smiled reassuringly. "I had similar questions at first, James. I have learned that these teachings come in layers, and we will find practical ways to apply them in our everyday lives, including managing stress and anxiety.

David, who had been sipping his tea, decided to share his thoughts. "I believe what we're learning here can help us maintain balance in our lives. Mindfulness, for instance, is a practice that I have been exploring, and it aligns with what Stuart was discussing. It's about being present in the moment, observing our thoughts and emotions without judgment."

Emma, who was nodding in agreement, added, "Absolutely, David. I've found that mindfulness has been a game-changer for me. It's like a tool that allows me to step back and respond to situations rather than react impulsively. It's a great way to manage stress.

Lori chimed in, "And when we combine mindfulness with what we learned about emotional frequencies today, it feels like we're getting a more comprehensive understanding of how to handle life's challenges."

Sophie, who was still feeling the effects of the audience's collective emotions from the demonstration, shared, "I think it's also about developing emotional intelligence. Understanding our own emotions and those of others can lead to more compassionate and harmonious interactions."

Kristol was happy with the lively discussion. "I couldn't agree more. It seems we can develop an understanding and apply these principles in our everyday lives. That, I believe, will make a real difference."

James, still wearing a skeptical expression, leaned forward. "I hear what you all are saying, and it sounds good in theory, but I'm struggling to see how this can help with my anxiety and stress. It's not like I can just flip a switch and change my emotional frequency, right?"

David responded gently, "James, I understand your skepticism. It's natural to have doubts when you're introduced to something new. What's important to remember is that change takes time, and it's a gradual process."

Sophie nodded in agreement. "Absolutely, James. It's not about flipping a switch; it's about awareness and practice. Small, consistent changes can lead to significant shifts over time. It's like building a muscle; it doesn't happen overnight."

Lori added, "And it's okay to have doubts. In fact, questioning and exploring are essential parts of the learning process. What matters is that you're here, open to exploring these ideas, and that's a great first step."

As the conversation flowed, Emma chimed in with a warm smile. "You know, James, tomorrow's session is about understanding the impact of emotions on our physical health. It might give you some more insights into how this can help with your anxiety and stress."

James looked a bit more hopeful at the prospect. "That sounds interesting. I've always heard that stress can wreak havoc on your body, so maybe there's something to this after all."

Sophie added, "Absolutely, James. Our physical health is closely tied to our emotional well-being. Learning how to manage our emotions can have a positive ripple effect on our overall health."

David nodded in agreement. "And sometimes, understanding the 'why' behind our physical symptoms can be a game-changer. It's all about connecting the dots between our emotions, thoughts, and physical sensations."

Kristol concluded, "So, James, maybe the answers you're looking for are just around the corner. I am here to support you, and I'm confident that you'll find valuable insights in the days to come."

James appreciated the reassurance and began to feel a glimmer of hope that this retreat might hold the keys to managing his anxiety and stress in a way he hadn't considered before.

The conversation at the dinner table began to wind down. The group shared their appreciation for the delicious, wholesome food that had been prepared for them.

Lori sighed contentedly. "I must say, this food is amazing." Sophie nodded in agreement. "Absolutely, Lori. It's like a feast for the soul as well."

As the plates were cleared away, Kristol looked around the table, feeling grateful for the connections. The day had been filled with eye-opening insights, and she couldn't help but feel a sense of anticipation for what the rest of the retreat had in store.

With a gentle smile, she said, "Well, it's been an incredible day. I think I am going to take some time for reflection. Tomorrow is a new day with more to learn and discover. I am going to take some time to write in my journal and prepare myself for morning yoga and meditation." She excused herself.

The next day arrived with the promise of more insights. With morning meditation and yoga complete, Kristol and Lori made their way over to the retreat center. With their journals in hand, ready to take notes about the topic of physical health and its connection to emotions, they walked into the center.

Stuart greeted them with a warm smile as they found their seats. He began by acknowledging the process they had made in understanding the mental effects of emotions.

"It's wonderful to see your enthusiasm," Stuart said. "Yesterday, we explored the mental landscape of emotions, and today, we're going to discuss how our emotions affect our physical health."

The group attentively listened as Stuart emphasized the importance of recognizing the mind-body connection.

He explained how our thoughts and emotions generate biochemical reactions within the body, affecting our overall well-being.

"As you've already learned, our emotions are like energetic frequencies that we emit from our bodies and subconscious minds," Stuart continued. "These frequencies have a direct impact on our physical health. Negative emotions can lead to stress, which in turn can manifest as physical ailments."

Kristol and Lori exchanged glances, both realizing the significance of this connection.

Stuart shared insights into how emotions such as anger, fear, and stress could trigger a cascade of physiological responses, from increased heart rate to the release of stress hormones. He also highlighted the power of positive emotions like joy, love, and gratitude in promoting physical well-being.

Stuart delved even deeper into the world of emotions, providing the participants with valuable insights. He began by highlighting the five fundamental emotions that underpin all human feelings: fear, anger, sadness, happiness, and love. These five core emotions, he explained, were the foundation from which a myriad of feelings and emotional states emerged.

"As we explore emotions," Stuart said, his voice carrying a sense of reverence for the subject, "it's important to understand that these five basic emotions serve as the building blocks of our emotional experiences. From fear, anger, sadness, happiness, and love, we generate a spectrum of feelings."

Kristol listened intently, recognizing the truth in Stuart's words. She reflected on how these core emotions had played significant roles in their own lives, shaping their thoughts, actions, and interactions with others.

Stuart continued to explain how each of these five emotions could give rise to a multitude of nuanced feelings. For example, fear could manifest as anxiety, worry, or insecurity, while anger might express itself as frustration, irritation, or resentment. Sadness encompassed feelings of grief, sorrow, and loneliness, while happiness could be experienced as joy, contentment, or elation. Finally, love, the most profound of emotions, extended into various forms such as compassion, empathy, and passion.

Stuart continued to unravel the intricate relationship between emotions and the human body, providing deeper insights into the physiological effects of each core emotion.

"Fear," Stuart began, "has a profound impact on our endocrine system. When we experience fear, our bodies release stress hormones like cortisol and adrenaline. These hormones prepare us for 'fight or flight' responses, but chronic fear can lead to imbalances in the endocrine system, affecting our overall well-being."

As Kristol listened, she recalled the fear in her life and became acutely aware of how it had manifested in her life, especially after the accident.

Stuart continued, "Anger, on the other hand, affects our digestive system. When we're angry, our bodies can enter a state of tension and stress. This can disrupt the normal functioning of our digestive organs, potentially leading to issues like indigestion, acid reflux, or even more severe digestive disorders."

"Sadness," Stuart explained, "has its impact on the respiratory and circulatory systems. When we experience deep sadness, it can lead to shallow breathing and a sense of heaviness in the chest. These physical manifestations are a direct result of the emotional state, affecting the health of our lungs and heart."

Stuart then shifted the focus to happiness, describing it as the doorway to opening the heart to gratitude and joy. "Happiness," he said, "affects all systems positively. When we are happy, our bodies release 'feel-good' chemicals like endorphins and dopamine. These not only boost our mood but also have a positive impact on our immune system, nervous system, and overall health."

The idea that happiness had a universal positive effect on the body resonated deeply with everyone, especially Kristol. She recalled the lessons that Citta had been teaching her.

Finally, Stuart touched upon love, describing it as a miracle healing frequency. "Love," he said, "has the power to harmonize our entire being. When we experience love, whether it's self-love or love for others, it creates a state of coherence within us. This coherence has a profound healing effect on our body, mind, and spirit."

Stuart encouraged the participants to take out their journals and pens and, with vulnerability and courage, confront their greatest fears.

Stuart began. "I want each of you to write down your greatest fear. It could be something you've carried with you for years, something that haunts your thoughts, or even a fear that has recently emerged. Be honest with yourselves."

Kristol, with her journal open and pen poised to confront a fear that had fought with in her subconscious for years, her fear of money. As she began to write, the words flowed from her heart, and her vulnerability spilled onto the pages of her journal.

"I've always had this fear," she wrote, "It's been with me for as long as I can remember. The fear of not having enough, of financial instability, of drowning in debt. It's a fear that has shaped so many of my decisions and actions throughout my life."

She paused, allowing the weight of her confession to sink in. It was a fear she had rarely spoken about, let alone acknowledged in such a raw and unfiltered manner.

"Growing up, I watched my family struggle with money," she continued. "There were arguments, sleepless nights, and a constant sense of uncertainty. I swore to myself that I would never let money control my life, but in doing so, I've allowed this fear to control me."

Kristol's pen continued to move across the pages, "It's not just the fear of scarcity," she mused. "It's also the fear of success. I've often held myself back, afraid of what might happen if I were truly successful. Would I lose touch with my values? Would I become someone I don't recognize? These questions have haunted me."

She concluded her journal entry with confidence. "I'm here at this retreat to heal, to transform, and to let go of this fear that has held me back for too long. I'm ready to face it, to understand it, and ultimately, to free myself."

Stuart continued, "Now that you've written down your greatest fear, take a moment to connect with it. Close your eyes, breathe deeply, and allow that fear to surface. Feel its presence in your body. Is it a heavy weight on your chest? A knot in your stomach or a tension in your shoulders? Pay attention to where in your body you feel this fear most acutely."

The room fell into a contemplative silence.

Kristol's connection with the fear of money intensified. It was as if she had opened the door to a long-forgotten chamber in her soul, and the emotions flooded in. Panic set in, and a cold sweat began to bead on her forehead and upper chest.

She could feel the fear's grip tightening, constricting her chest, and making her breathing rapid and shallow. It was an uncomfortable sensation, like a heavy weight pressing down on her, threatening to overwhelm her. She closed her eyes, focusing on her breath, and in that moment, she realized that the fear had taken residence in her upper chest, just above her heart. It was a physical manifestation of the emotional burden she had carried for so long.

Stuart's voice broke the silence. "Now, open your journals and write down where in your body you feel this fear. Be as specific as possible. This exercise is about bringing awareness to the physical manifestations of our emotions."

Stuart concluded the activity, "Remember, our emotions are not confined to our minds; they are woven into the very existence of our body. By acknowledging the physical impact of our fears, we take the first step toward healing and transformation."

Stuart guided the participants to explore the opposite of fear – love. He encouraged them to close their eyes, take a deep breath, and imagine what it felt like to be enveloped in love and warmth. They were asked to write down their sensations and emotions.

Kristol, her pen in hand, allowed her thoughts to drift to moments of pure love and joy in her life. She remembered the feeling of her mother's embrace when she was a child, the laughter shared with friends, and the unconditional love she felt for her dogs. As she wrote, a sense of warmth and lightness filled her heart.

Afterward, Stuart prompted them to pinpoint where in their bodies they felt the opposite emotion, in this case, love. She could sense a radiant, glowing energy in her chest, right where she had previously located the fear. It was as if the love had pushed away the darkness, filling her heart with a soothing, gentle warmth.

As she sat there, eyes closed, she realized the stark contrast between the two emotions. Fear had been a heavy, constricting presence in her upper chest, while love was a light, expansive energy that seemed to permeate every fiber of her being.

Stuart's words resonated deeply with Kristol as he continued his lecture. He explained that emotions existed on a spectrum, and if one emotion existed, so did its opposite. It was only our perspective and focus that sometimes led us to get stuck in one emotion rather than embracing the full range of human feelings.

Kristol couldn't help but drift off into her thoughts, recalling the conversation she had with Citta in the flower district. Citta had spoken about the duality of emotions, how fear and happiness could coexist, and how it was our choice where we directed our attention.

At that moment, it all seemed to connect. The fear she had just delved into, the panic, the sweat beads on her body – they were real, but they were just one side of the coin. On the other side was love, joy, and gratitude waiting to be experienced.

Stuart's lecture continued in the background as Kristol contemplated this realization. She understood that her perspective had often been stuck on the fear side of the emotional spectrum, specifically when it came to money and success. But now, she saw the possibility of choosing differently, shifting her focus toward love, abundance, and happiness.

The lecture continued as Stuart provided practical tools and exercises to help the students explore and embrace their emotions. They engaged in guided meditations and self-reflection exercises, allowing them to connect with their emotional core and gain insight into the intricate web of feelings that colored their lives.

As the lecture concluded, Stuart encouraged the participants to continue their journey of self-discovery throughout the retreat, and each day offered new opportunities to explore different facets of emotions.

Later that night, the group gathered for dinner in the dining hall. Fresh salads were served alongside baked salmon with a lemon dill sauce, roasted asparagus, and brown rice. Each dish was carefully prepared to elevate the body's vibration and promote overall well-being. The atmosphere was filled with a sense of openness, making it the perfect setting for a well-rounded conversation.

Lori took the initiative to start the discussion. She turned to James and asked, "James, how has your experience been in understanding and releasing anxiety and stress? Have you noticed how these feelings work in your body?"

James, who had been a bit skeptical at first, now appeared more contemplative. He nodded thoughtfully and replied, "Honestly, it's been eye-opening. I've always known I carry a lot of stress, but today's class made me realize how it physically affects me. I felt it in my gut, and I could sense that it's not a healthy state to be in."

Lori listened attentively to James, nodding in understanding. She replied with empathy, "I can relate, James. It's incredible how our emotions can manifest in our bodies. But the good news is that recognizing it is the first step toward healing and finding balance."

James leaned back in his chair, his skepticism apparent. "I get that this makes sense here, in this retreat setting, but I wonder if it's really possible to shift our emotional perspective long-term once we leave this place. Life out there is so different, with all its challenges and pressures."

David chimed in, offering a perspective of hope, "I think it's about practice and commitment, James. We're learning valuable tools here that we can apply in our daily lives. It won't be easy, but it's definitely possible to create lasting change."

The group engaged in a thoughtful discussion, exploring the practicality of maintaining emotional balance beyond the retreat's tranquil environment.

Emma chimed in. Today's class deepened my understanding of how emotions impact our physical well-being. It's like connecting the dots between what we feel and how our bodies react."

Sophie, who had been quietly observing the conversation, shared her perspective. "I've always been someone who's quick to react emotionally. Today made me realize the importance of pausing, taking a step back, and understanding why I feel a certain way. It's empowering to know that we have some control over our emotional responses."

Lori nodded in agreement and turned to Kristol. "Kristol, how have you been processing everything so far?"

Kristol took a sip of her water and sighed, her eyes reflecting on the intensity of her experience. "I have to admit, it was intense. Especially after my accident earlier this year." She started. "Connecting with my deepest fears and feeling them in my body has been quite overwhelming. It's like a floodgate of emotions."

Emma, empathizing with Kristol, "I can relate, Kristol. It's been a rollercoaster of emotions for me too. Facing those fears head-on can be daunting."

Sophie nodded in agreement, adding, "Absolutely, it's challenging, but it feels like a necessary step to healing."

James furrowed his brow, "I understand the idea of acknowledging our emotions, but do we really need to 'relive' them in this way? Isn't there a less intense way to work through them?"

David, who had been listening attentively, spoke next, "I think it's more about developing awareness of our emotions, not necessarily reliving them. By recognizing what's going on within us, we can choose how to respond and release what no longer serves us."

Lori nodded in agreement and continued, "Exactly, David. It's like shining a light on the shadows within us. We can't change what we don't acknowledge, right?"

Sophie added, "And sometimes, acknowledging those emotions, even if it's uncomfortable, can be a liberating experience. It's about taking control of our emotional well-being."

James pondered their words for a moment, seeming to absorb the perspective. "I see your point. It's just a bit overwhelming right now, but I guess that's part of the process."

Kristol interjected, "James, you're not alone in feeling overwhelmed. I feel overwhelmed myself. Today was an impactful day. I know I am tired."

The group felt a collective weariness as they finished their dinner, a full day of learning and self-exploration taking its toll. With a shared understanding, each of them looked forward to a peaceful night's sleep, knowing that they would awaken to a new day filled with opportunities for growth and transformation. Slowly, they made their way back to their respective rooms, ready to embrace the comfort of their beds and recharge for the challenges and revelations that lay ahead.

Chapter Sixteen

THE MONEY DANCE OF EMOTIONS

♥

Kristol awoke with a start, her body drenched in a cold sweat. Her heart pounded in her chest, and her breaths came in ragged gasps. It had been a night of vivid dreams, and they had plunged her into a visceral fear, forcing her to confront the very emotions she had been exploring during the retreat.

In her dream, she found herself standing at the edge of a bottomless abyss, surrounded by darkness. A shadowy figure lurked about, whispering taunts of doubt and insecurity. Fear, like an oppressive weight, pressed down on her chest, making it difficult to breathe. It was as if all her anxieties and worries had taken physical form in that eerie landscape.

As Kristol lay in bed, she realized that her mind was working diligently to process and release the deep-seated fear she had acknowledged earlier. It was a turbulent and uncomfortable process.

With a shaky breath, she reminded herself of the tools and techniques she had learned during the retreat. She gently placed her hand on her chest, feeling the rapid thud of her heart. Closing her eyes, she began to breathe deeply and slowly, focusing on each inhalation and exhalation. Gradually, her racing heart began to steady, and the icy grip of fear started to loosen its hold on her.

In the dim light of her room, Kristol reached for her journal and a pen. She needed to document this experience and capture the raw emotions and vivid imagery of her dream. Writing became a form of release, a way to externalize the fear and make it tangible.

As the words flowed onto the pages, Kristol could feel the weight of her fears lifting ever so slightly. She knew that healing was a process, and sometimes, it required facing the darkest corners of one's psyche. With each sentence she wrote, she reclaimed a bit of her inner strength and resilience.

In the midst of her distress, Kristol had a moment of clarity. She remembered the teachings from the retreat, the notion that if fear existed, so did happiness—it was just a matter of shifting her emotional lever.

With determination, she started working through the process she had learned, gradually releasing the fear that had gripped her. As she did, the heaviness in her chest began to lift, and she recalled the symbolism of the ridge on the quarter. It served as a reminder that she had the power to raise her vibration and transform her circumstances. Kristol was determined to elevate her emotional state.

Eventually, exhaustion overcame her, and Kristol returned to a restful sleep. She had taken a significant step forward that night.

The next day in class, Kristol arrived alongside the other students. Stuart welcomed the group with a warm smile, acknowledging the energy of the room. He could sense how the lesson from the day before sparked introspection with the students.

The session began with a round of questions and discussions, as Stuart encouraged everyone to share their thoughts and experiences. It was during this exchange that Kristol found herself raising her hand, ready to ask about her dream.

"Stuart," she began, her voice a little shaky, "last night, I had a really vivid dream that seemed to be related to our discussions about fear and emotions. It was intense, and I woke up in a cold sweat. I felt like I was facing my fears head-on in that dream. Is this a normal part of the process?"

Stuart nodded, his eyes filled with understanding. "Absolutely, Kristol," he replied. "Dreams can be powerful tools for processing emotions. They often bring to the surface the things we need to address and release. It sounds like your subconscious mind is actively working through your fears. Remember, our emotions are not confined to our waking hours; they can influence our dreams as well."

The other participants leaned in, intrigued by Kristol's experience and Stuart's response. Sophie, who had been sitting beside Kristol, chimed in, "I had a similar dream last night, too. It felt like I was confronting some deep-seated fears. It was unsettling but also strangely liberating."

Stuart smiled, acknowledging Sophie's input. "Dreams can indeed serve as a form of emotional releasing," he explained. "They allow us to access our subconscious mind more directly. What you both experienced is a sign that your inner selves are ready to address and release those emotions. Remember, when fear surfaces, you have what it takes to release and transform it. Otherwise, it wouldn't surface."

David raised his hand and added, "I had a dream as well, but it was more about embracing happiness and love. It was like a burst of positive energy."

"That's wonderful, David," Stuart said. "Dreams can also reveal the joyous aspects of our emotions. It's a reminder that our emotions are multi-faceted, and we can experience a wide range of feelings."

The day's lesson continued with Stuart ready to share the intriguing topic of the financial implications of emotions. "Today's topic," Stuart started, "is exploring how our emotions can have a significant impact on our financial well-being. Emotions, as we've discussed, are powerful energies that flow through us. They influence not only our mental and physical states but also our financial decisions and outcomes."

Stuart went on to explain that emotions could play a dual role in financial matters. On one hand, positive emotions like joy, gratitude, and love could attract abundance and financial prosperity. They created a positive energy field that drew in opportunities and resources. On the other hand, negative emotions like fear, anger, and a scarcity mentality could repel financial success, leading to poor decisions and missed opportunities.

"To understand this better," Stuart continued, "let's consider an example. Imagine two individuals, both facing a similar financial challenge. One person approaches it with a sense of fear and anxiety, constantly worrying about the lack of money. The other person, however, maintains a positive, optimistic outlook, believing that solutions will arise."

Stuart paused to let the scenario sink in before adding, "The person with a positive emotional stance is more likely to attract solutions, make wise financial decisions, and ultimately improve their situation. It's not just about wishful thinking; it's about the energy you emit into the world, which, in turn, influences the opportunities that come your way."

Kristol couldn't help but reflect on her own financial journey during Stuart's lecture. She recalled moments of financial stress and anxiety, which seemed to perpetuate a cycle of scarcity. At the same time, she recognized that her most prosperous periods had coincided with feelings of confidence and abundance.

Stuart continued, "Our emotions can also impact our spending habits. For instance, when we're feeling down or stressed, we might engage in 'retail therapy' to temporarily boost our mood. This can lead to impulsive spending and financial strain. Understanding the connection between our emotions and spending patterns is crucial to achieving financial balance."

Sophie raised her hand and shared, "I can definitely see how my emotional state has influenced my financial decisions in the past. It's like a lightbulb moment."

Stuart nodded in agreement. "Exactly, Sophie. Awareness of these patterns is the first step toward positive change. And we'll explore practical techniques to manage and redirect your emotions in the face of financial challenges."

As the lecture continued, Stuart shared how emotions had specific financial implications. Fear, he explained, could lead to financial paralysis, preventing individuals from taking necessary risks or seeking investment opportunities. Anger might result in impulsive financial decisions driven by frustration, while sadness could lead to emotional spending as a coping mechanism.

Throughout the lecture, Kristol diligently took notes, recognizing the impact emotions had on her money and security. She felt a growing sense of empowerment, knowing that with awareness and practice, she could make more conscious financial choices.

Stuart emphasized the importance of emotional intelligence on a soul level in financial matters. "By becoming more attuned to your emotions and their financial effects," he concluded, "you'll gain greater control over your financial destiny. It's incredible to see how our emotions and the words we use are interconnected with our financial well-being. These words have a profound impact on our financial reality, and understanding this connection can lead to transformative changes in our lives."

Stuart continued, "Money, in its essence, is an external energy form, while you, as an individual, are an energy form as well.

The key to understanding the dynamics between you and money lies in the realm of emotions and thoughts. Money, by itself, is neutral; it doesn't take action or have a response until it encounters the emotional frequency you apply to it.

It's like a mirror reflecting how you think and feel about yourself. Your relationship with money is a reflection of your self-worth, your beliefs, and your emotional state. If you send out negative or fearful vibrations, money responds accordingly, often by staying away or causing financial challenges. Conversely, if you cultivate positive emotions, abundance, and self-worth, money tends to flow more easily into your life. In essence, you are the one who shapes your financial reality through your thoughts, emotions, and intentions."

He continued, "Emotions and words carry vibrational frequencies that can affect our financial experiences. Take the word 'worthy,' for instance. When we feel worthy, it's as if we're increasing our net worth. This sense of self-worth directly influences the value of our financial assets."

Stuart went on, "Consider the word 'valued.' When we feel valued, it's like our bank accounts reflect that value. It's a reminder of how our sense of self-worth can impact the value of our financial resources. Feeling 'appreciated' is another intriguing word. When we appreciate the money we have, our accounts appreciate it in return. A lack of appreciation can negatively affect our financial assets and depreciate."

Stuart then explored the word 'enough,' saying, "Feeling 'enough' is powerful. When we believe we have enough to cover our needs and desires, we're sending a signal that we're content and satisfied with our financial situation. It's a sense of abundance in its own right."

He moved on to the concept of 'peace,' stating, "Peace in our financial matters is like claiming our 'piece of the pie.' When we find peace in our finances, it reflects positively on our financial outcomes. Balance is often mirrored in our financial balance. Striving for equilibrium in our lives creates a sense of balance in our bank accounts. It's about finding harmony in life between personal, professional, family, spiritual, and all our finances."

Stuart emphasized, "Feeling 'safe' is crucial. When we feel safe about our money, whether it's keeping it in a safe or securely in a bank, we're creating a sense of financial security. It's about the assurance that our financial resources are protected. And 'feeling secure' complements this. Money often represents a sense of security, and when we feel secure in our financial situation, we're strengthening the connection between our emotions and our financial well-being."

As Stuart wrapped up his lecture, the students sat in contemplation, realizing the impact that their emotions and words had on their financial lives in a way they never realized before. They understood that by aligning their emotions with positive words and intentions, they could harness the power of their thoughts to influence their financial reality.

"As we conclude our discussions today," Stuart began, "I can sense the incredible shifts happening within each of you. Tomorrow, we'll bring everything together on a spiritual level, focusing on the practical steps to make your own transformations."

He continued, "Our journey has been about self-discovery and empowerment, understanding that your emotions and intentions hold the keys to your financial well-being. Tomorrow, we'll explore how to consciously and intentionally shape your reality. It's about aligning your emotions, thoughts, and actions with your desired outcomes."

Chapter Seventeen

THE SUBCONSCIOUS SHIFT

As the group gathered for dinner, exhaustion was etched on their faces, but the wealth of wisdom they had gained about the financial implications of their emotions was priceless. Kristol, Lori, Sophie, Emma, David, and James took their seats, each contemplating the insights they had absorbed during their time at the retreat. The sense of unity among them had grown more robust with each passing day as they shared their personal journeys and discoveries.

Kristol, with her journal in hand, couldn't help but reflect on how her perspective had shifted since arriving at the retreat. She felt more connected to her emotions and their impact on her financial life. The fear that had once held her back seemed less and less, and she was beginning to see the potential for transformation.

Lori optimistically initiated the conversation as usual. "Can you believe how much we've learned about ourselves and our relationship with money in such a short time?" She looked around the table.

Sophie agreed. "It's been eye-opening, to say the least. I never thought that my emotions could have such a significant influence on my money."

Emma nodded, also agreeing, with her curly hair catching the evening breeze. "I always thought financial success was about making the right investments and decisions, but now I see that our inner world plays a crucial role, too."

James, who had been skeptical since the beginning of the retreat, admitted, "I still have some doubts about whether I can truly shift my emotional perspective when it comes to money, but I'm willing to give it a try."

With their plates nearly empty, Kristol felt inspired to deepen the conversation. She reached into her bag, retrieved her journal, and posed a question to the group that would ignite a meaningful exchange.

She asked, "As we reflect on what we've absorbed today, I would love to hear from each of you the most significant insight you have gained?" Kristol paused briefly, with her eyes focused on the flickering of the nearby candle, and she continued. "For me," she began, "the most eye-opening realization is how money serves as a mirror reflecting our inner world. It's incredible how the words we use to describe our soul level are so intertwined with our descriptions of our financial state."

Lori eagerly shared her perspective. "Absolutely, Kristol. I couldn't agree more. The alignment between our emotions, self-worth, and the state of our finances is fascinating. It's like our external world is a canvas painted with the colors of our inner landscape."

Sophie nodded in agreement, her eyes shining with new awareness. "It's not just about the numbers; it's how we feel about ourselves and how we relate to the world through our finances. Money becomes a reflection of our inner state."

Emma's face lit up as she joined the conversation. "What struck me is that transforming our financial reality isn't just about budgeting or investing; it's about healing and nurturing our relationship with money. It's about recognizing our worthiness of abundance."

David weighed in on the conversation. "It's true. Money isn't a separate entity; it's a mirror reflecting our thoughts and emotions. By changing our mindset, we can influence our financial reality. It's time that we take control of our inner world."

James was quiet, still a bit skeptical. Kristol asked, "What about you, James? What are your thoughts?"

"I used to see money as something external, almost beyond my control." James started, "Now I understand that it's intimately tied to my emotions and beliefs. It's empowering to know that I have more influence over it than I thought."

Kristol nodded, appreciating each person's unique perspective. "Money acts as a magnifying glass, amplifying our emotional states. If we're anxious, it magnifies that anxiety. If we're at peace, it reinforces that sense of security."

David, shifting the conversation a bit, "I can't help but think about how this journey is coming full circle. We started with understanding emotions and then moved to their mental and financial implications. Now, we're diving into the spiritual dimension. It's like each piece of the puzzle is fitting together."

Emma nodded, "Absolutely, David. It's like we're peeling back the layers of our inner selves, like an onion, uncovering the connection between our emotions and our spiritual essence. I can't wait to explore this final piece."

James thoughtfully shared. "I can't deny the shifts I've felt within myself. I'm genuinely curious to see how this spiritual perspective ties everything together. I'm beginning to believe that true transformation is possible."

"I couldn't agree more." Lori started. It's like we're about to unveil the grand finale. I have a feeling that understanding the spiritual connection to our emotions will provide the missing link we've been searching for."

Sophie added, "I've noticed that our discussions have evolved from the practical to the abstract. Clearly, our emotions are at the core of everything we've explored. I am curious how it relates to our spiritual nature."

Kristol smiled warmly at her friends. "You've all articulated my thoughts perfectly. Our journey has been a transformation of the heart, mind, and soul. And as we embrace the spiritual aspects of emotions, I have no doubt it will deepen our understanding and lead to lasting change."

Their discussion continued late into the evening as they shared their hopes and expectations for the final day of their retreat. They expressed gratitude for the insights gained, the friendships formed, and the anticipation of the spiritual lesson that awaited them.

As Kristol left the dinner table, she decided to take a leisurely stroll through the garden terrace. Under the starlit sky, with the scent of blooming flowers in the air, she felt a sense of unity and purpose. Kristol carried her journal with her, the pages filled with insights and wisdom from the retreat. She couldn't help but reflect on the lessons she had learned since her accident.

It was a wake-up call that genuinely changed the direction of her entire life. The dinner table discussion, what Citta had been teaching her about having your inner wisdom for financial success, the three sides of the quarter, and how your inner emotional state and the words that describe the soul's condition were often similar to those used to describe your financial well-being.

As she reached her room, Kristol opened her journal one more time, jotting down a few final thoughts. She felt a deep peace and clarity, knowing that she was leaving the retreat with a wealth of knowledge that extended far beyond financial matters.

The next morning dawned with a sense of anticipation. The students gathered for their regular yoga and meditation sessions, feeling more connected to their inner selves with each passing day. There was a shared excitement in the air as they sensed the promise of a full-circle moment, a day to align and integrate all they had learned.

After their morning practices, the group assembled for the final class on emotions and spiritual connection. Their hearts were open, and their minds receptive, ready to go deeper into the layers of understanding.

Kristol and her fellow students sat in a circle, ready for the day's final lesson.

Stuart started the session by acknowledging the journey they had all been on together. "Today," Stuart declared, "We bring everything together. We've explored the mental and emotional aspects of our physical health and financial lives. Now, we are going to discover how it impacts our spiritual lives and create a holistic transformation."

Stuart continued, "We've learned that emotions are the bridge between the physical and spiritual realms. Today, we'll focus on the power of emotions, a tool for manifesting our desires and aligning with our highest selves."

Continuing, "We explore the chakras today, the energy centers of our being, and how they serve as the bridge between the spiritual and physical realms. Each of us has seven main chakras, and these centers play a significant role in how we experience the world, including our financial well-being. It's crucial to understand that every chakra has both positive and negative aspects, and these energies influence every aspect of our lives, including money."

Stuart began with the Root Chakra, located at the base of the spine. "The Root Chakra represents our sense of safety, security, and stability," he explained. "When it's balanced, we feel grounded and confident in our financial matters, bringing in peace. The Root Chakra is also about our family, group consciousness beliefs, and the foundation that we stand on. But when it's imbalanced, fear and insecurity can take over, affecting our financial decisions with avoidance and procrastination."

Moving up to the Sacral Chakra, he said, "The Sacral Chakra governs our creativity, passion, and. expression of our emotions. The Sacral also is your relationship center to everything outside of yourself, including money. This is known as your 'Seat of Creation" and reflects having balance in all areas of life. We create from this center, including businesses. When it comes to your finances, this chakra plays a crucial role in how you manifest your desires. An imbalanced Sacral Chakra can lead to financial stagnation, blaming others for your decisions, and a lack of enthusiasm for financial goals."

"Moving on to the Solar Plexus Chakra," Stuart continued, "The Solar Plexus is your power center, governing your self-esteem, confidence, and personal power. This center is your 'sun center' and is your relationship to yourself. Truly your power center. When it's aligned, you feel a sense of control over your finances and the ability to make sound financial decisions. This brings an energy of pure joy and a state of energetic flow. An imbalanced Solar Plexus Chakra can result in financial insecurities and a fear of taking charge of your financial destiny. Judgment is often the culprit of having an imbalance here. Although we tend to judge things outside of ourselves, it is self-judgment that will stop the flow of money."

Stuart then directed their attention to the Heart Chakra, saying, "The Heart Chakra is the bridge between the lower chakras, which deal with the physical world, and the higher chakras, which connect us to the spiritual realm. When your Heart Chakra is open, you approach money with love, compassion, and generosity. An imbalanced Heart Chakra can lead to financial greed or emotional attachment to money. The opposite of love is hate, and this energy will quickly stop everything in your life from manifesting."

"A balanced Throat Chakra," shared Stuart, "resonates with generosity, as people find themselves naturally inclined to express gratitude and communicate their appreciation for the abundance in their lives. It encourages a mindset of sharing and giving back to the universe, knowing that such actions create a harmonious flow of prosperity. An imbalanced Throat Chakra can lead to behaviors that foster egotism. In this state, individuals may prioritize their ego-driven desires and elevate themselves at the expense of others. Their communication may be characterized by self-centeredness rather than genuine expression of gratitude or generosity."

Stuart acknowledged the class, making sure they understood all the concepts and continued the lecture: "The Third Eye Chakra, when balanced, serves as the seat of intuitive decision-making. It enables individuals to perceive the subtle energies and opportunities in the financial realm, guiding them toward choices that align with their highest good. A balanced Third Eye Chakra fosters a sense of clarity and insight, allowing individuals to make informed decisions that lead to abundance and fulfillment.

When the Third Eye Chakra is imbalanced, it can manifest as jealousy, greed, or envy in financial matters. Such imbalances cloud one's judgment, making it challenging to see the beauty in all situations, even when facing adversity. Instead of intuitive choices, individuals may be driven by ego-driven desires, hindering their ability to make sound financial decisions that promote overall well-being."

Stuart continues his lecture, reaching the last major chakra, The Crown Chakra. "In its balanced state, the Crown Chakra connects individuals to divine guidance in matters of wealth and abundance. There is a knowing and truth allowing you to align with your higher purpose. A balanced Crown Chakra keeps people focused on the present moment and open to receiving the wisdom and guidance needed for their financial success.

The imbalanced Crown Chakra can lead to feelings of regret, which tether people to the past. Such imbalances hinder your ability to access divine guidance and make conscious financial choices, preventing you from moving forward toward financial prosperity and spiritual growth."

Stuart concluded the lecture by reminding them, "Your chakras are the energetic gateways to your well-being. By nurturing and balancing them through the subconscious emotions, you can create a harmonious and prosperous relationship with money and health."

He led the group in a guided meditation, helping them connect with their inner emotions and desires. As they closed their eyes, Kristol felt a deep sense of calm wash over her. She envisioned her goals and aspirations, knowing that her emotions played a crucial role in bringing them to fruition.

After the meditation, Stuart encouraged everyone to share their insights and experiences. One by one, participants spoke about the emotional shifts they had experienced throughout the retreat and how these shifts had already started to impact their lives.

Kristol shared her own journey, describing how her fear and anxiety about money had held her back for so long. She spoke about the breakthroughs she had experienced and how she was now committed to rewriting her financial story with a new, empowering perspective.

Stuart nodded in approval and said, "That's the power of emotional alchemy. When we transmute our lower vibrational emotions into higher ones, we unlock our true potential. Remember, emotions are not good or bad; they're signals guiding us toward alignment or misalignment with our desires."

Stuart sensed the group's energy and readiness to take their knowledge to the next level. With a gentle smile, he began to explain the process of transforming blocked lower emotions into higher frequencies, effectively reprogramming their subconscious minds to manifest a different financial reality.

He asked everyone to close their eyes and take a few deep breaths. As they settled into a state of relaxation, Stuart guided them through the transformation process.

As the participants continued to breathe deeply, they focused on the merging of these two energies. The lower emotion began to soften and transform in the presence of the higher-frequency light. They felt a shift, a release, as the heavy energy of the lower emotion lightened.

Stuart guided them through this transformation, allowing them to experience the process of reprogramming their subconscious minds. They could feel a sense of liberation as the blocked emotion gave way to a more empowering and expansive feeling.

"Now," Stuart whispered, "imagine this transformed energy radiating from your heart center. Feel it expanding outward, creating a new vibrational frequency that aligns with your financial goals and aspirations."

The group continued to meditate, basking in the lightness and clarity. They could sense the shifts in their financial reality and emotional state, understanding that they held the key to reprogramming their subconscious minds and creating a different financial future.

"You have just experienced the transformational power of shifting your emotions," Stuart said. "Remember, you have the power to reprogram your subconscious mind and create a different reality in any situation you desire. Embrace this practice, and watch as a new world unfolds."

Chapter Eighteen

ENDINGS AND NEW BEGINNINGS

As the students gathered for their final dinner together, a bittersweet feeling hung in the air. They had come to the end of their transformative journey, and it was time to say goodbye to the relationships they had made.

Lori, Kristol, Sophie, Emma, David, and James shared stories and reflections from their time at the retreat. There was a deep sense of connection among them, a recognition that they had all grown and evolved together.

Lori raised her glass, offering a toast to the group. "To new beginnings and the changes we've experienced together," she said, her eyes filled with love. The clinking of glasses resonated throughout the room as they all raised their glasses in unison.

Kristol smiled, "I can't believe how much we've learned and grown in just a few days," she remarked. "I'll carry these lessons with me for a lifetime."

Sophie nodded in agreement. "It's been incredible," she said. "I feel like I've gained a new perspective on life and money."

Emma blurted out, "And the best part is that we can continue our friendships to support each other even after we leave here. We are together on this."

David spoke up. "I've learned so much about myself and how my emotions are connected to my financial journey," he said. "I'm committed to making positive changes in my life."

James added, "I came here looking for answers, and I've found a lot more than I expected. I'm excited to apply what I've learned and release the stress that's been holding me back."

The conversation continued, filled with laughter, gratitude, and a sense of closure. The group reminisced about their experiences, the classes, and the beautiful surroundings of the retreat center. It was a night of celebration and reflection.

As dinner came to an end, they exchanged contact information, promising to keep in touch and support each other. The realization of parting ways was a reality the following day, but they knew that the connections they had made would endure.

The following morning, they gathered one last time for breakfast, their suitcases packed and ready for departure. Hugs were exchanged, and promises to stay connected were reiterated. Each of them had been touched by the retreat and the insights they had gained.

With a final farewell, they headed their separate ways, carrying with them the lessons, the transformations, and the bonds that had been forged during their time together. They were all stepping into a brighter, more conscious future, ready to embrace their financial situations with wisdom and awareness.

As Kristol drove home, an inner peace stayed with her. The winding roads seemed to unfold before her like a painting through her thoughts. The wisdom she had gained was like a guiding light, illuminating her path ahead. She felt a sense of completeness and alignment she had never experienced before.

The hours on the road passed like a blink of an eye, and before she knew it, she was pulling into her driveway. Kristol greeted Liam with a radiant smile as he welcomed her home. The dogs, excited and wagging their tails, rushed to greet her, adding an extra layer of warmth to her return.

Liam looked at Kristol with a warm smile as she walked through the door. "Hey there, how was the retreat?" he asked, genuinely curious about her experience.

Kristol's eyes lit up as she replied, "Oh, Liam, it was incredible. It was like a healing transformation. I've learned so much about emotions, money, and life -- and how they're all interconnected. I feel a sense of peace I've never felt before."

He couldn't help but notice the radiant glow on her face and the sparkle in her eyes. "You look different, in a good way," Liam remarked, "There's something about you that's so... sparkly.

Kristol chuckled softly, feeling grateful for his observation. "I think it's the inner peace and clarity I've found. It's like I've unlocked a deeper understanding of myself and my relationship with the world. It's a wonderful feeling, Liam."

Liam nodded, appreciating the positive changes he saw in her. "I'm really happy for you, Kristol. It's amazing to see you so full of energy. I can tell that this retreat was truly transformative."

As they continued to chat about her experiences, Kristol couldn't help but feel grateful for the support of her friend. Liam gathered his belongings and his dog, bidding Kristol goodbye. He smiled and asked, "See you at the dog park next week?"

"Yes, of course." Replied Kristol. "I wouldn't miss it."

Kristol took a moment to sit on the sofa with her dogs, Max and Bella. She petted their furry heads and smiled as they wagged their tails in contentment. It felt good to be back inside the coziness of her home, feeling contentment. It was as if the retreat had not only transformed her understanding of emotions, money, and the role of fear. It also brought peace to her everyday life. She knew that returning to the corporate world and the realities of life would be a test, but she was equipped with valuable tools and insights to navigate it with grace and purpose.

After unpacking, Kristol settled at her desk, pen in hand, and began jotting down a to-do list for the next day. Her priorities included contacting her mother to let her know she was back home safely, catching up on some laundry, sorting the mail, and doing household tasks. Reflecting on her experiences, Kristol began jotting down her thoughts and insights in her journal, a new habit she had formed from the retreat.

As she settled into bed, she felt gratitude for the retreat and the positive changes it had already brought to her life. With a heart full of hope, she drifted off into a peaceful and restful sleep, ready to embrace the new day and the endless possibilities it held.

Kristol had a restful night's sleep, something that had eluded her for far too long. When she awoke, the sun was gently streaming through her bedroom window, casting a warm glow. Stretching her limbs, she felt remarkably refreshed.

With a smile, she padded over to the kitchen to start her day. Max and Bella greeted her with wagging tails. She let them out into the backyard, where they playfully scampered around, enjoying the crisp morning air.

While they were outside, Kristol prepared a fresh pot of coffee. The rich aroma filled her kitchen, signaling the start of a new day filled with possibilities. As she sipped her coffee, she contemplated her to-do list.

Picking up her phone, she dialed her mother's number. As the phone rang, Kristol thought about how much different she had felt since the retreat. Her mother's voice on the other end of the line was warm and welcoming. Kristol couldn't help but smile as they chatted, catching up on life and sharing stories.

"Kristol," her mother remarked, "your voice sounds different. There's something in your tone, a vibrancy I haven't heard in a while. It's… it's hard to put into words."

Kristol smiled on the other end of the line, touched by her mother's perception. "Mom," she began, "The retreat opened up a whole new perspective for me. I found answers to questions I'd been carrying for a long time, but it's not easy to explain it at all."

The conversation continued, with Kristol sharing some of the highlights of her retreat, like the beautiful surroundings, the inspiring teachings, and the wonderful people she had met. She kept the revelations to herself, knowing that they were deeply personal and still in the process of integration. Her mother listened attentively, sensing the positive changes in Kristol.

As Kristol was about to conclude her conversation with her mother, she heard a familiar and excited voice coming from the other side of her condo door. Without warning, Sarah burst into the room with an unmistakable aura of elation.

"Kristol!" Sarah exclaimed, barely able to contain her excitement. "Oh, my goodness, you won't believe what happened! I have been waiting all week to tell you. Thankfully, you are home now."

Kristol couldn't help but smile at Sarah's enthusiasm. She quickly said goodbye to her mother and hung up the phone, turning her full attention to her dear friend. "Alright, Sarah, you've got my attention. What's going on?"

"Remember when Matt Anderson asked about having me plan the Christmas Party, and I agreed? Well, as it turns out, they had me interview for a new position this last week and offered me a promotion!" Sarah exclaimed. "It's like a dream come true, Kristol."

Kristol's eyes lit up with genuine happiness for her friend. "Sarah, that's incredible news! Congratulations!" She moved closer to Sarah and gave her a warm hug to celebrate the achievement.

Sarah returned the hug with gratitude. "Thank you, Kristol! I couldn't wait to share this with you. You've always been my biggest supporter."

Kristol grinned. "And you've always been the hardest worker I know. You deserve every bit of this success."

Sarah's eyes sparkled as she glanced around Kristol's condo. "By the way, it's almost noon, and you're still in your PJs. Did you just wake up?"

Kristol chuckled, "Guilty as charged. I had a late night and a long drive back home."

Sarah playfully rolled her eyes. "Well, we can't have you lounging in your PJs all day, especially with this fantastic weather outside. Get dressed, and let's go out to celebrate."

Kristol couldn't argue with that logic. She headed to her bedroom to change while Sarah made herself comfortable in the living room. As she dressed, Kristol reflected on how her sense of peace and clarity seemed to be flowing into the lives of those around her, like Sarah's promotion.

As Kristol and Sarah prepared to head out to celebrate Sarah's promotion, Sarah couldn't contain another piece of exciting news that had been bubbling within her.

"Kristol," Sarah began, "there's something else I've been dying to tell you." Kristol raised an eyebrow, intrigued.

"Well, after that job interview, I had a little time to spare, and I decided to grab a coffee at a nearby café. And guess what? I met someone!"

Kristol couldn't help but grin at her friend's exuberance, her eyes lighting up. "Really? That's fantastic, Sarah! Tell me more."

Sarah continued, "We struck up a conversation while waiting for our coffee, and it turned out we have so much in common. We ended up talking for hours, and before we knew it, he asked if I'd like to go out for dinner."

Kristol's smile widened as she realized the significance of this moment for her friend. "That's wonderful, Sarah! I'm genuinely happy for you. What's his name?"

Sarah's cheeks turned slightly rosy as she revealed, "His name is Alex, and he's amazing. I haven't felt a connection like this in a long time."

Kristol couldn't help but tease Sarah gently. "Well, it sounds like things are moving pretty fast if you're already going on a date!"

Sarah's excitement bubbled over. "I know, right? But it just feels right, Kristol. I haven't felt this kind of energy in a while, and I'm ready." Sarah beamed. "I can't wait to see where this goes. And who knows, maybe I'll have some good relationship advice to share with you soon!"

Kristol laughed, knowing that Sarah was still the same person she had grown to love. Kristol and Sarah's day together was filled with catching up on each other's lives and indulging in some retail therapy. As they strolled through shops, Sarah couldn't help but share more about Alex.

"Kristol, you won't believe it," Sarah said as she showed Kristol a picture of Alex on her phone. "This is Alex, the guy I met at the café. He's such a sweetheart, and I can't wait for you to meet him."

Kristol examined the photo and smiled warmly. "Sarah, he looks like a great guy – and cute!"

Sarah's eyes sparkled with delight. "I have a feeling you'll really like him. We've been chatting non-stop since we met. It's like we've known each other for ages."

Their shopping spree continued, and as they browsed through stores, Sarah couldn't help but revisit the topic of Kristol's retreat. "So, Kristol, tell me more about this retreat you went on. It must have been quite an experience."

Kristol nodded, her mind drifting back to the transformative days at the retreat center. "It was, Sarah. It was more than I could have imagined. The retreat focused on our emotions, and I learned so much about how they affect every aspect of our lives."

Sarah listened intently, curious to hear more. "Wow! Can you give me an example?"

Kristol thought for a moment before responding, "Sure. You know how we often hear about the mind-body connection? We learned how emotions are not just thoughts or feelings; they're energy, and they affect our physical health, our relationships, and even our financial well-being and money."

Sarah raised an eyebrow. "That's quite a holistic approach. So, how do they teach you to work with your emotions?"

Kristol explained, "One of the key takeaways was that our emotions are like signals. They indicate what's happening within us. Instead of suppressing or ignoring them, we should acknowledge and understand them. It's about becoming aware of how our emotions affect our decisions and our lives."

As they moved from one store to another, Kristol continued to share her insights. "Sarah, imagine if we could identify the emotions that trigger our spending habits or the fears that hold us back from pursuing our dreams. The retreat taught us techniques to work with these emotions, to transform negative patterns, and to make more conscious choices into positive experiences."

Sarah nodded thoughtfully. "That sounds like something we could all benefit from. Do you feel like it will make a difference in your life?"

Kristol's gaze softened as she reflected on her personal journey. "Absolutely, Sarah. I feel like I've gained a deeper understanding of myself, and I'm more in tune with my emotions. Plus, having tools to reprogram, that is priceless."

Kristol returned home from her adventure with Sarah, still carrying the happiness she had cultivated during their time together. As she sorted through the mail, one particular envelope caught her attention—it was from the insurance company. Taking a deep breath, Kristol reminded herself to maintain her emotional state towards happiness, just as she had learned at the retreat.

She carefully opened the letter. To her astonishment, inside was a check that covered all of her medical expenses, hospital bills, and even the creditors she had been avoiding. The realization hit her like a wave of relief and gratitude, and Kristol couldn't contain her joy.

Tears welled up in her eyes as she realized the impact of her emotional transformation. It seemed that the universe had responded to her shift in energy and had provided a solution to her financial worries. Overjoyed and grateful, Kristol knew that this was a testament to the power of her understanding of emotions and their connection to her reality.

Chapter Nineteen

THE FOURTH SIDE

Kristol's return to work was met with a warm welcome from Seth, who couldn't hide his enthusiasm at seeing her again. He practically bounced over to her desk, a big grin on his face.

"Kristol! You're back!" Seth exclaimed. "You won't believe what you missed while you were away."

Kristol couldn't help but smile at Seth's excitement. "I'm sure I missed a lot, Seth. What's the latest office gossip?"

Seth leaned in closer as if sharing classified information. "Well, you know how Brenda from accounting and Jerry from IT have been secretly dating for months? Turns out, they finally came clean about it last week!"

Kristol smirked at the office drama. "Ah, office romance. That's always an interesting twist. Anything else?"

Seth continued to amuse her with tales of office happenings; however, Kristol noticed that while the stories were entertaining, they no longer held the same weight they once did. The petty grievances, office politics, and watercooler chatter seemed almost trivial in comparison to the knowledge she had gained at the retreat.

As Seth spoke animatedly about the latest office rivalry, Kristol found herself observing her surroundings with fresh eyes. The fluorescent lights, the buzzing of computers, and the constant chatter in the office—all of it was familiar, yet it felt different.

In the midst of Seth's storytelling, Kristol realized that although nothing in the office had changed externally, everything looked different from her new perspective. The retreat had opened her eyes to the deeper layers of life, the intricate dance of emotions, and the interconnectedness of it all.

She had learned to recognize the emotions that underpin her actions and decisions, and she was determined to navigate her work life with greater awareness. The office gossip, while entertaining, no longer held the same power to affect her.

Kristol couldn't help but feel the retreat transformed her outlook. It was as if she had been given a new lens through which to view the world, and she was determined to use it wisely.

Seth finally paused in his storytelling, noticing the thoughtful expression on Kristol's face. "Kristol, are you okay? You seem different."

Kristol smiled at her perceptive colleague. "I am, Seth. I've had quite an enlightening experience during my time away. It's made me see things in a new light."

Seth raised an eyebrow. "Enlightening, huh? Well, whatever it is, I'm glad you're back. We've missed you around here."

As Kristol settled back into her work routine, she knew the office gossip might continue; she had undergone a transformation that allowed her to approach it all differently. The world may not have changed, but Kristol had, and that made all the difference.

The week seemed to fly by in a blur of work and daily routines. Each moment was infused with focus and clarity, and Kristol found herself navigating life with a new direction and purpose. She had continued writing in her daily journal, jotting down her thoughts and reflections, which had become a cherished part of her daily routine.

As the weekend approached, Kristol realized that she had not seen Citta at the flower district in quite some time. It was as if the marketplace had taken a backseat to her new life.

Saturday arrived, and Kristol decided to visit the flower district, not only to soak in the vibrant colors and fragrances but also to seek out Citta. The moment Kristol stepped into the bustling flower marketplace, she felt an immediate shift in the atmosphere. The air was filled with the sweet symphony of nature, a harmonious blend of fragrances that danced around her. The vibrant colors of blooming flowers painted a picture of pure beauty.

As she wandered through the lively market, a sense of euphoria washed over her. It was as though the very essence of the flowers had infused her being with a renewed vitality and joy. The sun caressed her skin, casting a warm glow that seemed to match the radiance in her heart.

In the heart of the marketplace, Kristol spotted Isa's booth. With a radiant smile, Isa looked up and greeted Kristol, her eyes sparkling with warmth. "Kristol! It's been a while since I've seen you. How have you been, my dear?"

Kristol returned Isa's smile, feeling a lightness in her spirit that she hadn't experienced in a long time. "Isa, it's wonderful to be back here. I took some time for self-healing and was on a retreat."

Isa's laughter bubbled forth like a bubbling brook, filling the air with contagious happiness. "Ah, my dear, there's nothing quite like taking time for yourself, is there? And it seems like you've returned with a glow that matches the flowers around us."

As Kristol admired the intricate floral arrangements, she couldn't help but share her recent experiences with Isa. She spoke of her retreat, the clarity she gained, and the inner peace that now filled her days. Isa listened intently, her eyes reflecting a deep understanding.

"You know, Kristol," Isa began, her voice gentle and wise, "flowers have a unique way of mirroring our journey. Just as they bloom and flourish in their own time, so too do we uncover the beauty within ourselves when the time is right."

Kristol nodded, feeling a connection to the knowledge that Isa shared. She had always appreciated how the language of flowers transcended words, speaking directly to the heart.

As their conversation continued, Isa offered Kristol a bouquet of vibrant wildflowers, a symbol of the wild and untamed beauty that lay within each individual. Kristol accepted the bouquet with grace, feeling the energy of the flowers resonate with her sense of freedom and authenticity.

With the bouquet of wildflowers from Isa in hand, Kristol felt an anxious excitement bubbling within her as she approached the threshold of trees leading to Citta's sanctuary. Each step she took brought her closer to the wisdom and serenity she knew she would find there. The rustling leaves and the dappled sunlight filtering through the foliage seemed to beckon her onward.

The world around her continually transformed into a tranquil haven. Kristol's heart pounded with anticipation, and her spirit soared with the knowledge that she was about to reunite with Citta, the guardian of this sacred grove. She knew that their meeting would be a communion of souls, a sharing of insights and experiences that would deepen her understanding.

The world seemed to slow down, inviting her to savor the moment and relish the connection she would soon rekindle with Citta. She couldn't help but smile in anticipation of the friendship and conversation that awaited her beneath the sheltering canopy of trees.

Citta's presence radiated a tranquility that seemed to be an integral part of the sacred garden itself. As Kristol approached her, a warm smile graced Citta's face, and her eyes sparkled with recognition.

"How lovely to see you, dear Kristol," Citta greeted her with genuine warmth. "You look different as if a radiant light surrounds you."

Kristol felt a rush of appreciation and affection for the woman. She stepped closer to Citta, "Thank you, Citta," Kristol replied, her voice filled with sincerity. "I feel different like something within me has shifted. The retreat I attended was amazing, and I couldn't wait to come back here and share it with you." Kristol happily exclaimed.

Citta, with a graceful nod, her eyes never leaving Kristol's. "Nature has a way of nurturing transformation," she said, her voice carrying the wisdom of the ages. "It's wonderful to witness the changes that take place within those who are willing to experience its healing embrace."

Citta led Kristol over to a small wooden table and two chairs. The scent of earth and greenery filled the air. Taking their seats, Kristol couldn't contain herself any longer. "Citta, during the retreat, I learned so much about emotions, their impact on our lives, and the connection between our inner world and our outer reality."

Citta's eyes held a knowing twinkle as she gazed at Kristol. "Do you remember, Kristol, when you asked me about the wisdom to transform fear? Back then, it wasn't the right time, and I saw that you needed to have time for healing and growth. But now, from your commitment, dedication, and the experiences you've gained at the retreat, I see that you are ready."

Kristol nodded, reflecting on what had brought her to this moment. "Yes, Citta, I remember. I've learned so much about emotions, about myself, and about the power we hold within to transform our lives. Fear used to be a shadow that clouded over me, but now I feel more equipped to face it."

Citta smiled, "Transformation is a process, my dear, and it requires the right timing and readiness. Your journey has led you to a place where you can now embrace the wisdom to transform fear into strength, just as the caterpillar transforms into a butterfly."

Kristol leaned in, happily sharing her insights. "I realized that emotions are like the bridge between our spiritual and physical selves. They influence our thoughts, our health, our relationships, and even our finances. It's incredible how interconnected everything is."

Citta's smile deepened as she listened to Kristol's words. "You've grasped an ultimate truth, my dear. Emotions are the keys to unlocking the doors of our potential. When we learn to navigate them consciously, we become the architects of our destiny."

Kristol couldn't agree more. "And it doesn't stop there. We also explored the chakras and their role in our well-being. It's like each chakra is a gateway to a different aspect of our lives. When they're balanced, we're in harmony with the universe."

Citta's eyes gleamed with approval. "Indeed, the chakras are energetic centers that connect us to the greater cosmos. They are the conduits through which we receive and transmit energy.

Balancing them is the key to aligning with the universal flow and the transformative power of the human heart."

Her words hung in the air like a melodious whisper as she continued, "Remember, Kristol, how we spoke about the three sides of the quarter? Heads, tails, and the edge that connects them. There is a fourth side, hidden in plain sight and frequently overlooked. This fourth side is the space in between, where the magic truly happens. It is an inside-out approach."

Kristol leaned in, captivated by Citta's wisdom. "The space in-between, Citta? I've never heard of that."

Citta nodded, gleaming with ancient knowledge. "Indeed, my dear. This space in between is highly programmable, and it's influenced by the emotions and feelings that infuse everything. It's where vibration, frequency, and energy converge."

"Money is programmable? How does it work, Citta? How can we program this fourth side?" Kristol asked.

Citta's gentle laughter filled the air, "The programming of this fourth side happens through the emotions we carry within us and the intentions we set. When we infuse the space between ourselves with positive emotions, such as love, gratitude, and elevated intentions, we create a powerful energy field that ripples through our lives, infusing all things, including money. "

Kristol contemplated the implications of this revelation. "So, by nurturing our emotional well-being and intentionally infusing positivity, we can transform not only ourselves but also the world around us?"

Citta's smile held the wisdom of the ages. "Exactly, Kristol. The power lies within us to shape our reality through the fourth side, the space in between. When our emotions are aligned with our intentions and thoughts, we become instant co-creators of our destiny, and we can bring about positive change in our lives and the world."

Kristol's eyes sparkled with realization as she connected the dots between Citta's wisdom and her transformative experience at the retreat. "Citta," she began, "what you're saying about the fourth side of the quarter, it reminds me so much of what I learned at the retreat."

Citta nodded, her sage-like presence encouraging Kristol to continue.

"At the retreat, I discovered that our emotions, thoughts, and intentions are like the hidden fourth side of the quarter," Kristol explained. "Just as we often overlook that side, we tend to underestimate the power of our inner world. But as I went deeper into understanding my emotions and their impact on my life, I realized that this 'hidden' aspect holds the key to our transformation. I just didn't realize it infused everything around us."

Citta's warm smile acknowledged Kristol's insight. "Yes, my dear, it's all connected. Just as the fourth side of the quarter is the space in-between, the bridge between heads and tails, our inner world serves as the bridge between our current reality and the reality we wish to create. It's where the magic of transformation truly unfolds."

Kristol felt a sense of empowerment growing within her, fueled by the wisdom she had gained from both Citta and the retreat. "By nurturing positive emotions, aligning my thoughts with my intentions, and infusing my inner world with love and gratitude, I can program that 'fourth side' to manifest the reality I desire?"

Citta's eyes gleamed with pride. "Indeed, Kristol. You've grasped the essence of it. Now, you have the tools and understanding to continue shaping your destiny."

Just as the conversation reached a crescendo of understanding, a presence approached that gently diverted Kristol's attention. She turned her gaze toward the source and saw Isa approaching.

Isa's eyes intently sparkled as she approached and asked, "How is your meditation today?"

Kristol returned Isa's smile, her heart touched by the genuine interest of her friend. She took a moment to gather her thoughts, her eyes flickering with the remnants of the profound conversation she'd had with Citta moments before. "Meditation?" Kristol inquired. "I have been sitting here talking to Citta."

As Kristol mentioned her conversation with Citta, she turned her attention back to the chair across from her, expecting to see her wise mentor there. However, to her surprise, the chair was empty, and Citta was nowhere to be found.

A wave of confusion came over Kristol as she blinked in disbelief as if trying to grasp the reality of the situation. She glanced around, searching for any sign of Citta, but there was no trace of the sage-like figure she had been conversing with just moments before.

Her heart pounded with astonishment and bewilderment. Had it all been a vivid dream, a figment of her imagination? The deep insights and wisdom shared by Citta had felt so tangible, so real.

Kristol's mind raced as she contemplated the sudden disappearance of her spiritual guide. Was it a mystical encounter or a product of her own thoughts? She couldn't deny the transformation she had undergone during their conversation, the clarity she had gained, and the sense of peace that now dwelled within her. Isa offered a warm smile as she sat down next to Kristol.

"Kristol," Isa began, "what you experienced with Citta today is a beautiful reflection of the deeper truths that reside within you. Citta, in its essence, means the awakening of the mind-heart. It's not something external, separate from you, but rather the heart of the Buddha teachings that resides inside of you."

Kristol listened intently, absorbing Isa's words like a sponge. Her earlier confusion began to dissipate as she started to grasp the profound concept Isa was conveying.

"The insights you gained and the transformation you underwent during your conversations with Citta," Isa continued, "all of that came from the wisdom that lies within your own heart and mind. Citta is not an entity outside of you but a part of your very being, always ready to guide you on your path."

Kristol's eyes widened as she began to comprehend the depth of Isa's message. The realization slowly settled in that she didn't need to seek wisdom and guidance from external sources; it was already an inherent part of her existence.

Isa continued, "Citta teaches us that the answers we seek, the clarity we long for, and the peace we desire are not separate from us. They are woven into the very existence of our own consciousness. When we connect with our inner Citta, the mind-heart awakening, we tap into a wellspring of knowledge, wisdom, and compassion that can illuminate our path."

Kristol's voice trembled with both wonder and realization as she spoke, seeking confirmation of the extraordinary experience she had just encountered. "Isa, are you telling me that I was having a conversation with my inner self?"

Isa met Kristol's gaze with a reassuring smile, affirming the truth that had unfolded during their encounter. "Yes, dear Kristol," she replied gently, "what you experienced was a profound dialogue with your higher self, your inner Buddha if you will. It was a moment of deep connection, where you tapped into the wisdom and oneness that resides within all things."

Kristol's mind was abuzz with a mix of emotions—amazement, wonder, and a sense of discovery. She had always sensed that there was more to her existence than met the eye; however, this encounter had opened up an entirely new dimension of understanding.

Isa continued to elucidate the experience. "In your walking meditations, you were not only connecting with your inner self but also with the interconnectedness of all life, the oneness that flows through every living being, every blade of grass, and every whisper of the wind. It's a reminder that we are all part of a greater whole, and our inner wisdom is a reflection of universal wisdom. The universe is inside of you, reflecting out for you to experience."

Kristol took a moment to absorb Isa's words, feeling a deep resonance within her. It was as if the pieces of a puzzle she had been working on for so long were finally falling into place. The conversation with Citta, the realization of her inner wisdom, and now this explanation from Isa—all of it was integrating together.

Isa concluded with a heartfelt message, "Kristol, embrace the connection with your higher self, for it will continue to guide you towards greater understanding and inner peace. Remember, you are both the seeker and the source of wisdom."

As Isa spoke, Kristol felt a sense of empowerment and recognition growing within her. The mysterious disappearances of Citta were no longer a source of confusion but a lesson in realizing the inner source of wisdom.

Isa concluded, "Remember, Kristol, you carry the essence of Citta within you, and your journey of self-discovery is a lifelong adventure. Embrace the wisdom of your own heart and mind, and let it guide you towards the light of understanding and transformation."

Chapter Twenty

BUDDHA OF INNER ABUNDANCE

Feeling much reverence, Kristol turned her gaze to Isa.

"Isa," she began with a touch of hesitation, "would it be alright if I stayed here a bit longer? I feel the need to ponder all that I've learned today."

Isa's eyes, deep pools of understanding, met Kristol's with a gentle nod. "Of course, dear one," she replied kindly, "take all the time you need. The garden welcomes those seeking solace and contemplation. Reflect on the insights you've gained, for they are the stepping stones on your path to greater self-awareness."

Kristol closed her eyes and began to journey inward once more. The garden around her seemed to echo with the whispers of ancient wisdom, and in this sacred space, she continued to explore her own soul.

As Kristol sat, her mind began to travel back to the retreat she had attended, where she learned about the emotional impact of money, finances, and health and the different energy bodies the emotions affected. It was as if she had emerged from that experience like a caterpillar transforming into a butterfly, undergoing a metamorphosis.

She reflected on the powerful lessons she had learned during those transformative days. The retreat had opened her eyes to the intricate connection between her emotions and her financial well-being. Through the guidance of Stuart, Citta, and the wisdom of her fellow participants, she had come to understand that money was not just a tangible currency but a reflection of her inner state.

Reviewing her financial status, Kristol couldn't help but smile. She knew that all was well in her world. The anxieties and fears that had once gripped her when it came to money had given way to trust, faith, and unwavering belief. She had discovered that her thoughts and emotions were the architects of her financial reality, and she had chosen to build a foundation of prosperity, abundance, and gratitude.

Her true wealth went beyond material possessions; it encompassed a state of mind and heart. She had learned to release the limiting beliefs, emotions, and fears that had held her back. In their place, she had cultivated a mindset of internal wealth and success.

The emotional healing and transformation she had experienced were invaluable gifts that had enriched her life in ways she couldn't have imagined. She knew that she would always carry the lessons since the car accident with her as she continued to spread her wings and embrace the infinite possibilities of her newly awakened financial consciousness.

As Kristol sat immersed in her reflections, she opened her eyes and noticed something she had never seen before. There, in front of her, was a sign, weathered and rustic, but its message shone brightly:

> *Trust, and you will See*
> *Believe, and you will Know*
> *Have faith; all is Well*
> *Follow your Heart*
> *and Spirit will Lead you*

The words on the sign resonated deeply with Kristol, echoing the lessons she had learned during her transformative retreat experience and her time with Citta. It was as if the universe had placed this sign in her path, the truths she had come to understand.

She reached into her purse, retrieved her journal, and began to write down the mantra. The sign symbolized the core principles of trusting in herself and her inner wisdom, which had allowed her to see the world with new eyes, and her belief in the interconnectedness of emotions and finances, which had brought knowledge and clarity.

Having faith that all was well, even in the face of financial challenges, had been a powerful catalyst for positive change in her life. It was a reminder that trust, belief, and faith were the cornerstones of her financial consciousness.

The last line, "Follow your Heart, and Spirit will Lead you," encapsulated the essence of her lessons. Kristol had learned to listen to her heart's guidance and align herself with the universal flow of abundance. In doing so, she had felt a connection with her inner spirit, and it had indeed led her to a place of transformation and enlightenment.

With each word she wrote in her journal, Kristol felt a sense of deep gratitude for the experiences, teachings, and signs that had guided her. She knew that these lessons were not just for her but for anyone willing to trust, believe, and have faith in the infinite possibilities of life.

Kristol closed her journal with a satisfied smile. She took a moment to soak in the serene beauty one last time.

Picking up the wildflowers that Isa had given her, Kristol prepared to leave. The arching trees overhead seemed to bid her farewell with rustling leaves as if acknowledging the transformation that had taken place within her.

Turning toward Isa, Kristol smiled warmly. Their time together had been a gift. "Thank you, Isa," Kristol said, her voice filled with sincerity. "Your guidance has been invaluable to me. I will carry these teachings with me always."

Isa returned her smile with a knowing look as if recognizing the inner transformation that had occurred. "You were ready, Kristol, and you embraced it wholeheartedly. Remember that the wisdom you seek is always within you."

With a final nod, Isa confirmed, "Your time here was well spent. Go forth with an open heart and a spirit of adventure. Trust in yourself, and the path will unfold."

As Kristol left the flower stand, she couldn't help but be drawn to a stone Buddha statue sitting at a nearby booth. The expression on its face and the posture, with one hand resting on its heart and the other hand raised in a gesture toward the world, captivated her attention.

Approaching the statue, Kristol noticed something intriguing. On the hand that was raised in a gesture toward the world, there was a distinct symbol carved into the stone. It was a combination of two elements—a dollar sign ($) with a graceful arch beneath it, forming a harmonious and unique symbol.

Curiosity piqued, Kristol decided to inquire about the statue and the intriguing symbol on the palm of its hand. She made her way to the counter, where the friendly shop owner, a woman with a warm smile, was arranging bouquets.

"Excuse me," Kristol began, "I couldn't help but notice the beautiful stone Buddha over there with the unique symbol on its hand. It's such an interesting combination of a dollar sign and an arch. Does it have a special meaning?"

The flower shop owner paused for a moment as if savoring the question. She then turned her attention to Kristol with a kind and knowing look. "Ah, you have a keen eye for symbolism," she remarked. "That symbol represents a concept— the connection between inner and outer abundance."

Kristol leaned in with intrigue, eager to learn more. "Inner and outer abundance?" she repeated, seeking clarification.

The shop owner nodded. "Yes," she continued, "it signifies the idea that true abundance starts from within, from the heart. The dollar sign represents the external wealth and material prosperity that many seek, but it's the arch beneath it, a Tao symbol, carries the deeper message. It symbolizes the inner journey, the path of self-discovery, and the realization that wealth, in all its forms, is a reflection of what lies within."

Kristol absorbed this insight with a sense of resonance. It echoed the teachings she had received during her transformative retreat experience. "So, it's a reminder that our inner state, our beliefs, and emotions are intricately connected to our external abundance?" she inquired.

The shop owner smiled warmly. "Exactly," she affirmed. "When we cultivate inner abundance—love, gratitude, compassion, and a sense of oneness—it radiates outward, attracting external abundance in various forms, including financial prosperity. It's a beautiful reminder to tend to our inner gardens as they ultimately bloom in the world."

The shop owner, recognizing Kristol's genuine interest, reached behind the counter and retrieved a small tag with a description of the Buddha statue. She handed it to Kristol with a gentle smile. Kristol took the tag and read the description with curiosity:

> *"Buddha of Inner Abundance*
>
> *This exquisite stone Buddha embodies the profound connection between inner and outer wealth. With one*

hand resting on his heart and the other reaching out to the world, this statue symbolizes that true abundance begins within.

The symbol carved into the hand signifies the flow of energy—representing both the external wealth we seek and the internal treasures we cultivate through self-awareness, love, and compassion.

This Buddha is a sacred reminder that your inner state shapes your external reality. Let it inspire you to nurture the garden of your heart, where the seeds of abundance are sown."

Kristol paused, letting the words sink in. She felt a deep resonance with the message and the symbolism of the Buddha. It was as if the statue itself had chosen her.

Kristol couldn't resist the deep resonance she felt with the Buddha of Inner Abundance. She knew that this statue was not just a beautiful piece of art; it was a sacred symbol of the transformation she had undergone.

She looked back at the shop owner and smiled. "I would like to purchase this Buddha," Kristol said, her voice filled with certainty. The shop owner nodded at the significance this statue held for Kristol. She carefully wrapped the Buddha and placed it in a box.

As Kristol made the payment, she felt the synchronicity that had brought her to this moment. It was as if the universe itself had guided her the entire way. With the wrapped Buddha in her hands and the tag safely tucked away, Kristol started walking through the flower district a final time to leave.

Kristol was lost in thought, her mind still filled with thoughts. As she walked, she meandered through the busy flower district, almost in a dreamlike state; she was not fully aware of her surroundings.

Then, as if the universe had a way of orchestrating synchronistic encounters, she turned a corner and collided with someone. Startled, she stumbled back slightly, and a familiar face came into view. It was Benjamin, the man she had encountered twice before, at the office Hawaiian party and the corporate office.

Their eyes met, and there was a moment of recognition between them. Benjamin's face broke into a warm smile, and he extended a hand to help Kristol regain her balance. "We seem to have a habit of running into each other," he said with a chuckle.

Kristol couldn't help but smile in return, feeling a sense of serendipity in their repeated encounters. "It does seem that way," she replied. "I suppose the universe has its plans."

Benjamin nodded, his eyes thoughtful. "Perhaps it does," he mused. "I've always believed that sometimes when we're open to it, life has a way of guiding us in unexpected directions."

Kristol found herself nodding in agreement. "There is a truth in that, I have recently learned. What are you doing here in the flower market?" Kristol inquired.

Benjamin replied, "I came here to purchase flowers for my mother's birthday, but if you're free," he paused, "would you like to join me for a cup of coffee?"

Kristol smiled, feeling a genuine connection with this man she had literally run into three separate times. "I'd like that," she replied. "It seems our paths keep crossing for a reason."

Benjamin offered to help her with the Buddha and flowers; they made their way to the café. Kristol couldn't help but feel that this encounter with Benjamin was a piece of the puzzle, another synchronistic connection.

As Benjamin and Kristol entered the café, the aroma of freshly brewed coffee filled the air. They settled into a quiet corner, their conversation becoming more engaging by the minute. Unbeknownst to them, this chance meeting was about to unlock secrets, ignite passions, and unveil mysteries that would challenge their perceptions of reality, leaving them on the brink of a life-altering journey they never saw coming.

MEET THE AUTHOR

Dawna Campbell

Dawna Campbell, known as "The Mind Whisperer," has been a transformative force for over 25 years, specializing in emotional healing and personal transformation. She is a renowned speaker, author, and retreat host, dedicated to empowering individuals to lead lives filled with emotional abundance, optimal health, and enriched relationships.

Dawna's career path has been a unique blend of financial expertise and holistic healing. Before founding her company, The Healing Heart, Inc., she served as the Managing Principal of an investment firm, managing portfolios exceeding $500 million in assets. This financial background provided her with a deep understanding of the financial challenges individuals and businesses face, which she combines with her passion for emotional healing.

Dawna's expertise lies in reprogramming the subconscious mind for emotional and financial well-being, a skill that has earned recognition in over 135 media outlets. Her transformative work has helped countless individuals break free from emotional constraints and achieve lasting emotional and financial prosperity.

Dawna's mission is to create a better world through heart-centered healing, helping individuals unlock their true potential, manifest their dreams, and lead lives filled with emotional abundance, financial prosperity, and well-being.

If you would like to schedule a free consultation with Dawna, you can visit her website at www.bettercalldawna.com or bring her to inspire your organization, see her Speaker Media Kit at www.bookdawna.com. To learn more about Dawna, visit at https://www.dawnacampbell360.com/contact-dawna.

The Mind Whisperer

FINANCIALLY FIT
TRANSFORMATION

Release Stress and Chaos in life
Ignite Unstoppable Inner Confidence
Expedite your Results

HolisticLIFE
Recognition as the
Financial Mindset Program of The Year 2023
Financially Fit
Dawna Campbell

If you spent years working towards your potential financial future, and you are still not there - the answer is within you - literally

DAWNA CAMPBELL

Made in the USA
Middletown, DE
15 October 2024